ARMSCOTE MANOR
BOOK OF
DRIED FLOWERS

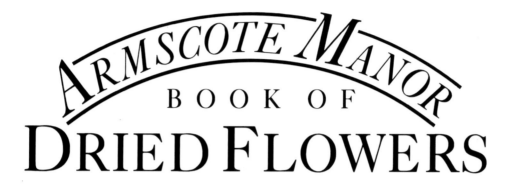

ARMSCOTE MANOR
BOOK OF
DRIED FLOWERS

AMANDA DOCKER

Flowers with Simon Lycett

CENTURY

London   Sydney   Auckland   Johannesburg

Design by Polly Dawes
Photographs by Julie Fisher
Styling by Jacky Boase

First published in 1990 by Century Editions an imprint of The Random Century Group Ltd,
20 Vauxhall Bridge Road, London SW1V 2SA

The Random Century Group Australia (Pty) Ltd,
20 Alfred Street, Milsons Point, Sydney, NSW 2061, Australia

The Random Century Group South Africa (Pty) Ltd,
PO Box 337, Bergvlei 2012, South Africa

The Random Century Group New Zealand Ltd,
PO Box 40-086, 32-34 View Road, Glenfield, Auckland 10, New Zealand

British Library Cataloguing in Publication Data
Docker, Amanda
Armscote Manor book of dried flowers.
1. Dried flowers. Flower arrangements
I. Title
745.92

ISBN 0-7126-3718-4

Typeset by SX Composing Ltd, Rayleigh, Essex
Colour separation by Colorlito, Milan
Printed and bound in Spain by Printer Industria Gráfica, Barcelona

PROP ACKNOWLEDGEMENTS

The author and publishers are grateful to the following companies for
the loan of items used in the photographs for this book.

James Davis
Pine and Country Antiques
28 Church Street
Shipton-on-Stour

Gallery of Antique Costume and Textiles
2 Church Street
Marylebone
London NW8

For Fred, who is such a great business mentor, guide and motivator, and my patient and understanding family — especially my mother, whose garden I've robbed of flowers on many occasions.

ACKNOWLEDGEMENTS

Grateful thanks are due to the many people who have made vital contributions to this book, but especially to:

All my wonderful friends who so kindly allowed us into their homes – Jane Brabyn, Dominic and Sally Cadbury, George and Caroline Docker, Robert and Fiona Grant, the Sandiford family, Michael and Louise Wigley, the Reverend Roger Williams, rector of St James the Great, Idlicote and last (but not least!) Charlie and Julie. Thanks, too, to Karen Abel-Smith for help in finding locations.

The Armscote Manor Dried Flowers workforce, who took all requests in their stride. Special thanks to the invaluable Mary Davis, who always keeps everything running smoothly, to Mick for solving so many practical problems and to Liz in the office.

The floristry team who helped with and inspired so many of the arrangements – the brilliant Simon Lycett, Antony Mifsud who created the arrangements on pages 37, 61, 62 and the central arrangement on pages 20-21, and David Greenwood and Annie Daniels.

Everyone who supplied materials for the arrangements, including Lady Beecham for the wonderful artichokes, Kari Dill for leek heads, Hamish Greycheap for the splendid Christmas tree, Jenny Henstock and Anne Davenport for their lovely stone and terracotta pots and Miss Williams for the honesty.

James Davis of Pine and Country Antiques for lending us so many antiques.

Gyles and Michele Brandreth for getting the whole project off the ground.

Julie Fisher and her assistants for the lovely pictures, Jacky Boase for styling them and Mary Douglas for help with writing and transport.

June for all the lunches and bed changing!

And, finally, to my family for putting up with all the disruption during the making of this book.

CONTENTS

A WALK AROUND ARMSCOTE MANOR   10

The Flowers of the Field   12

AROUND THE HOME   20

Kitchens and Corners   22

Making the Arrangement: Becher's Brook   30

Country House Style   32

Town Meets Country   56

Making the Arrangement: A Daisy Tree   68

OUTDOOR PERSPECTIVE   70

Exteriors   72

Out of Doors   79

Making the Arrangement: A Rope Garland   82

SPECIAL OCCASIONS   84

A Winter Wedding   86

Making the Arrangement: A Bride's Headdress   94

An Easter Celebration   96

A Harvest Festival Supper   101

Making the Arrangement: A Year-Round Decoration   114

A Cotswold Manor Christmas   117

Making the Arrangement: A Christmas Tree   126

A RESOURCE GUIDE   128

Drying Your Own Flowers   130

Equipment and Materials   134

Suppliers of Dried Flowers   135

A Plant Lexicon   140

INDEX   142

A WALK AROUND ARMSCOTE MANOR

Armscote Manor is set in the gently rolling countryside of the northern Cotswolds, surrounded by gardens that have scarcely changed since the house was built at the end of the sixteenth century. Today, as well as being our family home, it's the centre of one of the largest dried-flower businesses in Britain. In the barns and outhouses around the stableyard are workrooms where flowers are transformed into arrangements and sold the world over. Let me introduce you to the place and its history, and to some of the people who live and work there . . .

Armscote Manor, our home and the inspiration for our dried-flower business. In the foreground is a selection of the arrangements we make there.

THE FLOWERS OF THE FIELD

The little history we know of Armscote Manor begins in 1587, when John Halford inherited the original house and its lands from his father. Armscote must have taken the latter part of its name from the sheep-cotes that dotted the fields all over the area that, because of them, became known as the Cotswolds. In the sixteenth century Cotswold wool was considered the finest in Europe and it was probably on wool that the Halfords' fortunes were founded.

During the 13 years between inheriting the manor and the end of the century, John Halford built the house that my husband Fred, my children Sophie and William, and I live in today. When he carved his initials into the oak front door the wood must have been new and still soft enough to be worked. Nearly 400 years later it is black and hardened with age, but his initials are still there.

There are other strands from the past that reach out to us across the centuries. While John Halford was building his new house at Armscote, a local man, William Shakespeare from Stratford-upon-Avon, just ten miles up the road, was making his name in London. Today, I need hardly point out, Shakespeare is still Stratford's biggest claim to fame.

Another link that I like to imagine ties the house as it is now to the house as it was then, concerns Halford's wife. When the Halfords moved into their home they would very probably have used dried and preserved flowers to scent the rooms. Perhaps Mrs Halford and her servants spent their summers drying herbs and lavender, which would have been burnt to perfume the house when dampness made it musty – the word 'perfume', incidentally, coming from the Latin meaning 'through smoke'. Perhaps she collected petals from the rose garden at the back of the house and used them to make the delicious moist potpourri, at that time literally a 'putrid pot', that was the precursor of today's dry potpourri. Maybe she dried sprigs of tansy, wormwood, rosemary and lavender and hung them in bunches in cupboards to deter moths from the Cotswold woollens. Indeed she may have dried other garden flowers so that they could be used to brighten the house during the long, dark days of winter.

I hope she did, because it pleases me to think that after four centuries dried flowers still play a significant part in the life of Armscote Manor. True, our closets don't contain bunches of wormwood and rosemary to keep away the moths, but our rooms are perfumed with potpourri and we still, each year, dry roses, lavender, herbs and many other flowers picked from the gardens the Halfords knew. Whether this traditional use of flowers was observed throughout the intervening years, we'll unfortunately never know. The Halfords lived quiet lives and quiet lives tend to be overlooked by history.

Armscote is said to have provided a hiding-place for Guy Fawkes, who attempted to blow up the Houses of Parliament in 1605. Unfortunately he is said to have stayed in so many other houses in the area that it's something of a local joke.

History does, however, record one incident that occurred at the manor on 17 December 1673. The generation of Halfords then living at Armscote were religious non-conformists and when George Fox, founder and

Hollyhocks outside the front door where John Halford, the man who built Armscote Manor, carved his initials. My companion is Teal, our golden retriever.

leader of the Quakers, was travelling from London to his home in the North of England they offered him accommodation at the manor. That evening a meeting was arranged and so many local people flocked to attend that it had to be held in the barn. Fox tells the story in his journal:

We . . . went to John Halford's, at Armscot in Tredington parish, where we had a very large and precious meeting in his barn, the Lord's powerful presence being amongst us.

After the meeting, Friends being most of them gone, as I was sitting in the parlour, discoursing with some Friends that staid, one Henry Parker, called a justice, came to the house, and with him one Rowland Hains, a priest of Honington, in Warwickshire.

Parker and Hains arrested Fox and took him to Worcester Jail, from where he was later released to continue his work. The incident was never forgotten, however, and to this day local Quakers commemorate the event by coming to lunch at Armscote on the first day of August each year and walking in the gardens where Fox once walked. The Halfords' faith may well explain why we know so little about them. As Quakers they would have pursued neither fame nor fortune – and it is perhaps as a consequence of the latter that the manor eventually passed out of their hands.

It came into ours in 1977, in need of restoration after an unsympathetic Victorian treatment that had tried to conceal the real character of the place. Fred and I lived in a cottage nearby for a year while the architects and builders did their best to uncover what original features remained. The fireplaces were still there, and some of the flagstones, but we never quite managed to work out which area would have been the high-ceilinged Elizabethan hall that is so characteristic of houses from this period. We moved in just before our son, William, was born.

Having found ourselves a beautiful home, Fred and I now had to work out a way of keeping it. With the house

had come 16 acres of land and a full-time gardener, both of which needed to be put to good use. Fred is the business brains of the family, and his entrepreneurial instincts guided us in the direction of dried flowers. We decided to grow and dry our own and make them into arrangements which we would then sell by mail order. And I would be in charge of the day-to-day business.

Becoming a businesswoman was the last thing I had anticipated and not a prospect I welcomed with much warmth. Before our marriage I'd worked with horses and they were my only real interest outside the family. My idea of a good time was (and still is) to go riding or salmon fishing in Scotland. Business meetings, spread sheets and cash-flow projections were not something I felt terribly confident about, but with Fred's constant guidance and assistance, Armscote Manor Dried Flowers was established in 1979.

Not the least of my concerns was the fact that I had no training in floristry. Many people assume that I'm a professional or that at the very least I'd gone to the kind of school where flower arranging was taught. I didn't, and qualifications in Maths, Zoology and Geography were not much use when it came to designing our first products. Fortunately we were lucky to find a very skilled and imaginative florist living in the next village and she helped us tremendously. It was from her that I learned all my basic skills. I'm sure now that it was an advantage not to have been formally trained. If you don't know the 'rules' of

Off to another Pony Club gymkhana. My children have inherited my love of horses and we often spend our weekends riding. Here's Sophie with her pony Bruni and William with Minnie. Unfortunately Fred was too busy mucking out the horse box to be in the picture.

Fiona, one of our wonderful team of arrangers, making a special commission in the workroom

dried flower arranging, then you have no inhibitions about breaking them!

The early years of the company were exciting and, sometimes, disastrous. Our gardener certainly knew how to grow the flowers we needed, but we had frequent problems with fields of flowers destroyed by rain or mildew. On one memorable occasion a whole crop of helichrysums was wiped out by leatherjackets. Setbacks aside, the fields full of flowers were a glorious sight and it was wonderful to be out on summer mornings picking them – even if our gardener's idea of a practical joke was to fasten my brimming basket to the ground with a length of wire so that when I tried to pick it up everything fell out!

The barn that we converted to a drying shed was a magnificent sight, with racks of flowers strung up to the ceiling and everywhere great masses of colour and foliage. Helping to run all this and turn the dried flowers into finished arrangements was a team of workers recruited from the local area.

From these small and perhaps unlikely beginnings, the business grew. We reduced the amount of trade done through mail order because of problems with packing and transporting the individual arrangements and instead began selling in bulk to retailers. As the number of orders grew, so did the problem of producing enough flowers for them. An ever-increasing amount of material had to be brought in from outside and we needed extra space to store it. As word of us spread, local arrangers and shops began asking if we could supply them with flowers. People began to call at the manor to buy arrangements or to ask us to make special commissions for them. If our business was to expand, we would have to make some changes.

Reluctantly we decided that it simply wasn't practical to go on growing and drying our own materials. We needed the barn for more work-rooms, and to create a

A small sample of the flowers and materials on sale at the Armscote Manor shop. We stock flowers to suit all tastes, including exotic proteas and banksias, but our best-sellers are traditional pink roses. When we started the business in 1979 there was a relatively limited range of flowers available. Today exotic material comes to us from all over the world. We in turn export our arrangements throughout Europe and to places as far afield as Barbados, Bermuda, the United States, Japan and even the Falkland Islands.

showroom and shop where our flowers could be displayed. It's rather sad that today's arrangements aren't made from flowers grown at Armscote, but we still have local people who supply us. Ewan Evans is the most remarkable of our suppliers. He grows and individually wires up all the helichrysums we use – and we use lots. He also cooks a brilliant breakfast when he comes with us to trade fairs! Other friends kindly grow or collect other sorts of material, including such things as artichokes and onion heads. One of my mother's friends collects fir cones and larch twigs for us, invaluable for our Christmas arrangements.

The fields around the manor may no longer be full of flowers, but the garden certainly is, and most of them can be dried. Every year I cut armfuls of each variety and hang them in the kitchen or, when there are too many to cope with there, in the loft above the work-rooms. When they are dry I use them for my own arrangements.

We regularly arrange evening visits to Armscote for groups who are interested in dried flowers and when the weather is good enough I begin by inviting them to walk around the gardens with me. As we go I point out all the materials that can be dried. Later we return to the work-room for a demonstration and there I sometimes make an arrangement incorporating dried flowers from one of the flowerbeds we have just seen. Our visitors often go away full of new ideas and plans for their own gardens. If you are interested in growing flowers to dry, I've drawn up a list of the most common and suitable garden flowers on page 140. And on page 130 you will find details of the various methods that can be used to dry them. It's worth doing, even though it's so easy to buy commercially-grown dried flowers. There's something very satisfying about making arrangements from materials you have cultivated and preserved yourself.

We are planning some changes in the garden. To one side of the house is the old, walled, kitchen garden. We call it the moon garden because one way of entering it is via a circular archway, like a moon. Here we used to grow flowers for havesting, but for the last year or two it has been allowed a rest from intensive cultivation. It's here that we are planning a show garden of annuals, perennials and everything that can be grown for drying. The traditional English garden flowers – peonies, delphiniums, the different varieties of roses, poppies, achilleas, alchemilla, hydrangeas, sedum, anaphalis and on down an almost endless list – will be cultivated and we may also attempt to grow some of the more exotic and unusual plants that can be dried. We hope that this will provide our visitors with some extra inspiration.

I'm sometimes asked about my personal preferences when it comes to flowers. Personally I love informality; wild flowers, herbs and old-fashioned garden flowers, fresh or dried, are my favourites. I like natural, loose-looking bunches and arrangements with lots of seed heads and contrasts. Often the simplest arrangement, perhaps a container filled with just one variety of flower, can look spectacular. I admire the flair of European arrangers, who are more bold and daring than the traditional English school of floristry, which tends to stiffness and pointed triangular shapes. That said, I'm not a great fan of the wildly modern, brightly-coloured arrangements one sees in Europe, full of dyed flowers and odd accessories. Like so many other English people I love a natural, informal style of gardening, full of soft, rich colours and shapes, and I prefer my flower arrangements to echo that style.

It delights me that after so many years of decline, the art of producing and arranging dried flowers has made its comeback. For centuries people preserved and dried flowers to create a reminder of summer through the long winter, but in this century the practice seemed in danger of dying out. One of the most encouraging developments since Armscote Manor Dried Flowers began trading has been the huge increase in the varieties of flowers available on the market, with new additions every year.

Of course, no dried material can rival the delicacy of fresh flowers. A solitary dried rose will never arouse quite the same feelings as a perfect fresh one. But there's tremendous satisfaction to be derived from preserving the beauty of flowers by drying them and then making them into a wonderful arrangement, a permanent reminder of their impermanent beauty.

Whilst a bunch of beautiful fresh flowers needs very little effort to make it look good, dried flowers require more time and, most of all, inspiration. All too often, even today when there are so many excellent dried-flower suppliers around, people's idea of an arrangement is a few hydrangeas grouped with some statice or honesty in a vase. No one could begin to pretend that this kind of treatment does anything to enhance the look of the flowers, the vase or the setting. For dried flowers to look their best they need to be selected and arranged with a theme or an idea in mind that has been inspired by the setting in which they will be seen. In this way the flowers, setting and container will complement each other and the arrangement becomes not just a decoration, but an important and beautiful feature of the room.

To demonstrate how this works in practice, I'd like to take you on a tour of the lovely Cotswold homes of my friends and family and show you some of the magical qualities of dried flowers and the tremendous variety of materials available for use. If you're new to flowers and flower arranging don't be put off by the terrifying Latin names accorded to some of the plants. Wherever possible I've used their more familiar titles, but certain species are only known in their Latin form, so in these instances, I've had to give the Latin. On the journey I'll explain the sources of our inspiration and the thinking behind the arrangements. I'll outline the basic skills involved and pass on the tips I've learned over my years at Armscote Manor. I hope what you see and read will inspire you to make new and imaginative arrangements of your own. Forget the rules, the traditional colour combinations and the established ways of doing things. Just follow your creative instincts and enjoy the results.

CHAPTER TWO
AROUND THE HOME

Dried flowers are often viewed in a purely practical light, as nothing more than a convenient way of decorating a stark corner or a bare piece of furniture. But used with imagination they can become a beautiful and integral feature in the design of any room, and give enduring pleasure throughout the year. Come with me to visit the homes of some of my friends and let me show you how dried flowers make them such beautiful places to live . . .

Dried flowers are the perfect complement to the mature colours and textures of old terracotta tiles and mellow wooden furniture

KITCHENS AND CORNERS

According to some authorities dried flowers aren't a practical proposition in kitchens, utility rooms and other places around the house where water, steam, intense heat and bustling activity create exactly the kind of conditions guaranteed to ruin them. And certainly, if your kitchen steams up each time you boil the kettle, or is so small there's nowhere but the draining board on which to put an arrangement then you're unlikely to find that dried flowers last long or look good.

But as I know from my own experience, some kitchens can be ideal locations for dried flowers. At Armscote we're fortunate enough to have an Aga, an absolute godsend for anyone who likes to dry their own flowers. There's usually a whole rack of flowers freshly cut above mine, and when they're dry – often just a matter of a few days – I hang them in bunches from the beams across the ceiling until they're used. In summer we breakfast under roses, peonies, alchemilla and artichokes, to name just a few of the things I pick from the garden. At other times of the year visitors find herbs and greenery gently drying over their heads.

Many kitchens in older country houses, my own included, face north and can be rather gloomy. But what's bad news for the cook is good news for dried flowers, for they keep their colour best when they're out of direct sunlight. Nothing could suit them better than a shady kitchen with plenty of dry heat, and they'll do wonders for the look of the room, particularly if it's decorated and furnished in a country style.

There can be few more delightful kitchens than the one shown on the previous page. The owners of the house are great Francophiles who love the warmth and simplicity of Provençal style and have recreated it in their Oxford-shire home. This is the kind of kitchen in which dried flowers are indispensable, and we created three highly individual arrangements to complement its character.

On the left of the picture is a tall basket, loosely filled with dried herbs including rosemary, bay, lavender, marjoram, tansy, curry plant, feverfew, borage, catmint, sage and chive flowers. They were all freshly dried, having been picked only a week or so earlier, and were pungent enough to scent the entire room and give it an earthy, appetizing aroma. We picked the herbs at a growers' not far from Armscote and discovered that the flowers are usually cut and thrown away because they cannot be processed. If you'd like a similar arrangement of your own but don't have a herb garden, you might try approaching your local herb nursery and asking if you may pick a few armfuls of flowers. You may find that you're doing them a favour.

Heads of garlic and *bouquets garnis* were wired over the rim and down the sides of the basket, adding to the aromatic dimension of the arrangement. The technique for attaching the garlic or, indeed, any other type of fruit or vegetable, is quite simple. Run a heavy-gauge florists' wire (see page 134) through either end of the bulb, twist the wire firmly round the base of the garlic to hold it in place, and then thread the ends into position through the basket and secure. For an almost instant transformation of a plain basket, ready-made plaits of garlic can be wired around the edges, as demonstrated in the picture. Garlic will look good for many months until it dries out and discolours, at which point it can easily be replaced with new bulbs. With the *bouquets garnis* it's an important addition to this design not just because of its aroma but because it helps break up the line between the basket and the flowers to create an attractive and fully integrated arrangement.

On the low painted chest, beneath the flying angel, is an intriguing arrangement made of twigs and knobbly-textured banana sticks, with a green background of carthamus. It's like a fantasy tree, with walnuts, pecan nuts and tiny terracotta flowerpots, only an inch or two in diameter, clustered among the branches, while larch cones, tamarind husks and the muted pink *Protea sulphurea* add colour and texture at the base. This is a fun arrangement, eccentric and eclectic, full of new discoveries each time one looks at it. Gnarled old apple twigs would make an equally interesting framework for the arrangement, and one could fill the small pots with dried-flower heads for a softer and more colourful approach. Dried acorns and prickly chestnuts would also look good.

Seeking inspiration for the third arrangement, we asked ourselves what kind of images were conjured up by thoughts of a warm country kitchen. Freshly baked bread came immediately to mind – and there it was, our theme. I find this kind of brainstorming technique immensely useful when I'm searching for new ideas. Even if the first idea that comes to you doesn't appear to have anything to do with dried flowers, it's worth trying to incorporate it into an arrangement. You may be pleasantly surprised at the results.

We filled an old terracotta breadcrock (borrowed from my mother and still, I confess, to be returned) with upright wheat stalks. Then a moss garland was attached around the rim of the crock using strong florists' tape (see page 134), which is invaluable for fixing materials to solid containers that you don't want to damage. If you're attaching a garland permanently and aren't concerned about damaging the container then use glue – if possible hot glue, applied with a glue gun, which gives the best adhesion. Into the garland were wired a number of bread rolls

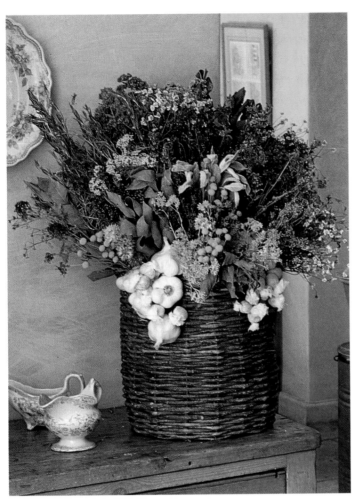

Few arrangements could be more appropriate in the kitchen than dried herbs, which fill the room with a pungent and pleasing fragrance. Grow your own herbs for drying or ask a herb grower if you can cut flowers in the summer.

Imagination and wit — two of the key words when it comes to creating truly original designs. Here, bread rolls and kitchen implements transform a very simple arrangement into something that's different, fun, and perfect for its setting.

of different shapes and sizes. Bread will last almost indefinitely in an arrangement as long as it is kept in dry conditions, otherwise it will go mouldy. If you want to preserve it allow it to dry in the air for a few days and then spray it with clear varnish. Then we added an assortment of small and interesting kitchen implements. Our housekeeper, June, arrived for work the next day to discover that most of her wooden spoons had mysteriously disappeared. A sugar shaker, pastry cutters, cornet tins, little madeleine moulds and butter pats were all included. To finish the garland off, small bunches of wheat were interspersed among the utensils, hiding any wires and providing a visual link with the sheaf above.

I should, perhaps, sound a light-hearted note of caution about arrangements incorporating edible materials such as the loaves used here. Be careful if you have hungry dogs (or even, for that matter, hungry children) about. We left this arrangement, complete with bread, on the kitchen floor overnight. Teal, our golden retriever, was unable to resist the temptation, and when we came down in the morning all the rolls had gone.

Kitchens aren't the only functional rooms in the house that can be dressed-up with a dried arrangement. This hall-turned-boot-room, for example, made an excellent setting for one of the standard arrangements we produce at Armscote. I call it the Becher's Brook because the twig-covered basket and shape remind me of the formidable steeplechase fence of the same name in the Grand National. It is one of our best-selling styles and popular, I suspect, not only because it looks good but because it is narrow and flat-backed, which makes it useful for placing against walls. This is a particular bonus in narrow halls and landings, where there's less likelihood of it being knocked over by someone accidentally brushing past.

There's not much danger of that happening here,

The Becher's Brook, one of Armscote Manor Dried Flowers'
specialities. Narrow, flat-backed arrangements such as this are ideal for
hallways and passages, where deeper arrangements might be brushed by
people passing by.

however. Most boot rooms are terrible, pokey little corners, full of discarded footwear, muddy jackets and broken bits of pony tack, places in which dried flowers would be wasted. Something that could never be said of this boot room, and the Becher's Brook arrangement complements it entirely, managing to be both decorative and functional. Because it's such a distinctive and adaptable arrangement, I've shown how to make it in detail on page 30.

Another attractive, but practical, arrangement we put together was the design for the turn in the narrow stairs that lead from this room. It had to be an informal, country-style design – no neat baskets. We found a large copper pan that seemed to fit the stairs nicely and then chose a pretty but fairly bright selection of flowers to fill it. The material, including oats, flax, amaranthus, helichrysums, Russian statice and green honesty, was arranged quickly using chicken wire as a base, and inserted in clumps to see what the basic effect was like. As it turned out, this deceptively relaxed style gave us precisely what we were looking for.

Becher's Brook and the other arrangements we've seen all take a little time and effort to make. But for the very simplest ways of using dried flowers, I'd like to return to the kitchen. It seems to me that of all the rooms in the house, this is the place where very simple dried arrangements can be used most effectively. Formal drawing-rooms usually require something on a grand scale: bedrooms are best suited to neat, pretty designs and for the

The simplest and most informal of arrangements in an old copper pot – but even informality has to be planned before you begin work. The choice and size of container had to be right to fit this awkward turn in the stairs.

dining-table one looks for something formal and elegant. In the kitchen, however, there are opportunities for small bunches, loosely-packed baskets of hedgerow flowers and generally more informal types of presentation. But even these simple arrangements have to be used and constructed with a sense of style. All too often one sees haphazard and mismatched combinations of flowers jammed carelessly into badly-prepared containers – a few lanky grasses sticking their heads above a couple of hydrangeas, finished with a spray of sea lavender or gaudy statice protruding at an odd angle, stems displayed, and with no sense of proportion, shape or form.

You don't need exotic flowers or home-grown roses or herbs to make something look eye-catching. You don't have to spend hours making moss garlands and wiring-up bunches. With just a little style sense you can take a handful of grasses, drop them into a jug, and have an almost instant arrangement to be proud of. Naturally I'd like to encourage everyone to be more adventurous and use dried flowers in new and imaginative ways, but I also recognise the attraction of sheer simplicity. So here are my three rules for absolute no-nonsense dried-flower arrangements with a little class.

1 The paler and less interesting the contents, the more colourful and imaginative the container should be.

2 Always arrange the flowers in a smooth, rounded shape, never in a point or spikes.

3 Use enough dried material to fill the container and keep the contents in shape. Never leave gaps.

As you can see from the wonderful country kitchen shown on page 28, if you follow the guidelines you can end up with some very lovely arrangements. The attractively-shaped old basket adds form to a low-key, country-style combination of yellow achillea and quaking grass. The blue jug sets off another neatly mounded bunch of the

This kitchen has so much colour and fascinating detail to catch the eye that flowers are best kept simple. But simple doesn't have to mean boring. A strictly limited number of shades arranged in attractive containers create strong shapes which attract the attention quietly and blend harmoniously with their setting. The wooden cats, the details of the crockery and painted shutters, the flowers and the texture of the ochre-coloured walls are all shown to their full advantage.

same grass. These simple arrangements can be replaced or adapted in a matter of minutes when they become faded or dusty, or when you become bored with them. They provide a changing contrast to the equally simple but larger arrangement on the windowsill. Here a well-proportioned terracotta pot houses a beautifully-shaped arrangement of rust-coloured dudinea and verticordia. This just goes to prove that you don't have to do anything fancy to achieve a really impressive result. There are no wires, clever colour combinations or dramatic contrasts of flower forms, just a good container and a strong, uncomplicated shape.

At the top of the picture you'll see another way to create an effective and reasonably-priced display – a full hop bine, twisted around a beam, with sprays of dudinea and preserved mimosa tucked into it to add colour and warmth. If you have a suitable ceiling beam or doorframe to drape it over, a hop bine makes a dramatic addition. Hammer a few small nails into the wood and use wire to tie the bine in position.

An equally uncomplicated method was used to decorate the wonderfully-carved wall cabinet. Bunches of flowers, taken directly from the Armscote shop, were tied with raffia and suspended from each side. We chose a combination of interesting textures and colours, using both exotic and typical British species. On the left, at the top, are the bristly brown seed heads of one of the banksias, natives of Australia. Beneath it is a cloud of alchemilla and below that the pretty pink and blue seed heads of nigella. At the bottom are the silver-blue spikes of sea holly that we grow most years at Armscote. To the right, the vaguely reptilian scales of *Nervosum verticor*, a South African exotic, create an interesting focal point against the plain bunches of barley and oats. Tying and hanging the bunches was the work of a few minutes. The result? Extra colour, texture and interest that shows off the cabinet all the better.

Hanging bunches – the easiest and quickest way of decorating an isolated cupboard or dresser. And when one gets bored with the original bunches, they can be replaced by new ones with the minimum of expense and trouble.

Making the Arrangement
BECHER'S BROOK

Becher's Brook is an excellent arrangement for a beginner to attempt. It looks impressive, yet its formal construction – straight rows of flowers at different levels – means there's little chance of going wrong. Its flat-backed style makes it the ideal arrangement for setting against a wall.

The most difficult part of making a Becher's Brook is selecting the flowers. You will need a variety of tall, spiky material for the back and softer, shorter flowers for the front. Choose your colours by making sample swatches of different combinations, and don't be afraid to try out a few unlikely contrasts. For the container you need a long, narrow basket constructed of twigs. Don't worry if it has a handle as this will be hidden by the flowers. These are available from a variety of shops, from department stores to specialist florists' suppliers (see page 135). If you have difficulty in finding one, or if you wish to make a larger version of the arrangement like the one shown in our boot room picture on page 25, you can trim an ordinary woven basket with twigs or off-cut stems. Simply form the stems into small bundles and secure them vertically to the basket with U-shaped wires. When the basket is covered add a horizontal trim to hide the wires. For a more elegant variation, though not a true Becher's Brook, one could use a fish kettle or other similarly-shaped container.

MATERIALS REQUIRED
● *A long, narrow basket*
● *Dry foam blocks*
● *Stub wires*
● *Scissors and a knife*
● *A selection of flowers (in this example I used amaranthus, pink larkspur, alchemilla, roses, glixia, dahlias and hydrangeas)*

1 Cut the dry foam blocks to fit the basket. Push U-shaped wires through the basket and into the foam to hold it firmly in place. Use another U-shaped wire to hold the foam blocks together.

2 Start at the back using the tallest material. I used green amaranthus for the back row, with pink larkspur in front of it. Be careful not to place the material too close to the edge of the foam as it may break.

3 Complete one end of the arrangement so that you can work out the best proportions and how far each layer should drop below the previous one. When you are happy with this, finish the rows. Tough-stemmed material can be stuck straight into the foam, but tiny flowers or those with flexible stems will have to be wired into bunches first.

4 The flowers for the bottom row of the arrangement should be inserted so that they cover the top of the basket and conceal any glimpses of foam. Hydrangeas are ideal for the purpose.

COUNTRY HOUSE STYLE

I find country house style almost impossible to define, and yet I think most of us know what we mean when we use the phrase. For me it creates visions of eclectic collections of old furniture and treasures; traditional fabrics and colours, sometimes faded and worn; a sense of comfort and warmth, though not at the complete expense of elegance, and a feeling of continuity with the past, an ease and maturity born of time.

Flowers, of course, form an integral part of this vision and have always been an important part of country house life, both figuratively – in fabrics, papers, carvings and paintings – and literally. At Armscote I use fresh flowers in many of the rooms, but I don't always have the time to make a really exceptional feature of them. It's unfortunate, because houses like Armscote are at their best when they are full of flowers. Yet they could be, simply by introducing a few dried-flower arrangements.

I'm not going to pretend that dried flowers are a replacement for fresh ones. I believe that both should be treated very differently and valued for the specific qualities and advantages they offer. It's true that dried flowers lack the delicacy and grace of the fresh material, but it's equally true that most fresh flowers need daily attention and last for perhaps only a few days. Ideally one should use both, to ensure that whatever the season and however busy one is, there are always flowers of some kind in the house.

The lovely manor house home of my brother-in-law and his wife, Caroline, is always full of flowers. She has a bold and highly skilled sense of design and colour and for their living-room, pictured on page 33, she chose warm shades of tangerine and burnt orange. To make any kind of impact at all our arrangement had to be just as bold in colour.

The brightest highlights are supplied by the Chinese lanterns and the zinging scarlet-orange tones of the dahlias, with their ruffled petals. Orange-tufted carthamus also makes an important contribution. The light, sharp green of its foliage was a particularly good combination with the orange shades and we followed it up by choosing yellow-green alchemilla and spikes of amaranthus for contrast. To prevent the overall effect from becoming too heavy we added bunches of pale oats and quaking grass, with several shades of dyed gypsophila, some fronds of dark bracken and, for textural variation, the large, bristly heads and serrated leaves of Australian honeysuckle. Tucked in, here and there, are sprigs of dudinea and glixia in sympathetic shades. This arrangement offers a splendid splash of colour to the room when placed in a prominent position, and when there's time for fresh flowers it can be moved to a less central spot where it will brighten up a dull corner.

From the living-room we move into the dining-room. I must admit that I'm not really surprised that so many people have forsaken the formal dining-room for the cosiness of the kitchen. Grand dining-rooms are fine for special occasions, but for everyday use they're often quite impractical. And, because they're seldom used they

A classic basket arrangement of brilliant orange dahlias and Chinese lanterns makes a warming contribution to a living-room. Dahlias are quite unusual and much nicer, I think, dried than fresh. For a little exotic texture we added a couple of bristly Australian banksias with their distinctive serrated leaves near the base of the arrangement.

tend to have a rather chilly and unlived-in feel when the time does come to get out the monogrammed silver and the crystal. Anything one can do to add colour helps, and one sure way is to use dried flowers. They can be left, untended, during those periods when the room is unused, and will look fine on their own for Sunday lunches or informal occasions. For something more grand try combining them with fresh flowers for a really full effect.

Not all dining-rooms are chilly and unlived in, of course. In fact chilly is the very last word one might use to describe the one pictured here. It is warm, welcoming and just one of many bold, beautiful and comfortable rooms in a quite glorious manor house not far from Banbury in Oxfordshire. I'm fortunate enough to have been a guest here, and it really is the most remarkable place for a dinner party.

When it came to designing a dried-flower arrangement for such a setting, our first challenge was to attempt to define the colour of the panelling and walls. A sort of maroon, we agreed at first. Then the sun came out and opinions were divided. Brick red and rust red were volunteered for the main colour of the walls, and a crimson red suggested for some of the details. We realized that there was going to be very little chance of matching the colour and that it was best not to try.

A bold, beautiful dining-room.
When you are designing
flowers for a room decorated
in a strong and subtle colour,
like this one, it's easier and often
more effective to look for contrasts
than to try and match shades.
The basket in the fireplace is a
good example of how this can
work spectacularly well. The
strong blues, pinks and green
bring out the best from the rusty-
red walls.

It was a wise decision and one which I would advocate to anyone else facing a similar problem. Materials that match a room's colour scheme can give you initial confidence when starting an arrangement, but if you get too obsessed with colour co-ordination the end result can be flowers that echo their background so closely that they almost disappear. The nearest match we found for this room was red capucin leaves, a few of which can be seen in the basket in the fireplace. Unfortunately when we tried using them in the smaller arrangements they had a rather depressing effect and had to be removed. Faced with this there was no alternative but to look for contrasts. We decided, after a few experiments, to pick up the secondary colour of the curtains, blue, and strong violet-pink. The results were certainly not boring.

Many of us own attractive glass and silverware that is rarely used and seldom seen. I like the idea of putting these items to use in the dining-room, where they seem most at home. Better to have them full of dried flowers than gathering dust or looking empty and forlorn on the side-table. By the fireplace is a glass bon-bon dish containing a simple arrangement that includes green amaranthus, pink roses and peonies, blue larkspur and the distinctive soft red of leptospermum, commonly known as silver strawberry.

When making an arrangement in a glass container, it's advisable to line it first so that the plastic foam, wires and other fixings are invisible from the outside. This isn't always necessary if one is using cut glass because the patterns obscure the contents, but I always think it's worth doing anyway. For the bon-bon dish we used potpourri, which had the added advantage of perfuming the room. One can just as easily use moss, leaves, lavender or flat flower heads. To fix the foam inside the container we used strips of florists' tape (see page 134). As I have said before, this is the only method I would suggest if you're using cut

glass or any other precious container that mustn't be marked or scratched.

The low arrangements on the table were made in two silver dishes, which were first lined with thick black polythene to prevent scratches from the wires. Again, the foam was held firmly in place with a few strips of florists' tape stretched across the top. The flowers include lavender, nigella, pale pink peonies, pink dudinea and flax, which has tiny, nodding, ball-shaped heads with subtle touches of pink and purple. It's a robust and interesting way of softening an arrangement, much better than sea lavender or gypsophila. The dishes were finished with pieces of sphagnum moss tucked around the edges to hide any glimpses of foam that might have been reflected by the shiny table.

For the centrepiece we used a delicate silver epergne with four glass flutes. It's the ideal container for this situation, with enough height and character to attract attention, yet not so tall and bulky that it dominates the table and blocks the view of the diners. I greatly appreciate the opportunity of using antique pieces like this, which might otherwise have spent most of their lives hidden in the back of a cupboard. If they are filled with dried flowers you can keep them proudly on display, knowing they are making a positive contribution to the setting.

Each of the epergne's glass flutes was lined with potpourri and filled with small pieces of plastic foam, then arranged with the same selection of flowers that were used in the low dishes. These arrangements are simple rounded shapes, easy enough for even a beginner to tackle and very quick to complete. Rather more demanding and time-consuming is the large basket in the hearth, which uses the same colours and flowers as the table arrangements but includes a few extra additions, such as sharp-green amaranthus and rusty-red capucin leaves. I think it helps to have one large design like this in a room where there are a number of smaller arrangements. On their own the smaller arrangements may look bitty and lost, but if they are seen in conjunction with larger features they become part of an integrated scheme.

Other ideas for decorating a formal dinner-table might include a wide, flower-filled garland that runs the length of the table. Use large flowers such as hydrangeas, delphiniums, peonies and celosia to bulk it out, with mimosa and glycerined ivy (see page 131) to trail attractively across the table.

For a luxurious talking point, why not wire some beautiful fruit into the garland? Mouthwatering purple figs and blue-black grapes, trailing brambles covered in blackberries, the glossy autumn colours of pomegranates, pinkish lychees, bright orange kumquats and wrinkled passion fruit – they would all look superb. For a variation on the same theme, make individual arrangements of dried flowers and fruit in small bowls or terracotta pots and use one to decorate each place setting. At the end of the meal guests can be invited to help themselves to fruit from the arrangements.

The setting for the next two photographs, shown on pages 38-9 and 40, is one of the most idyllic of all the houses you'll see in this book. It belongs to a family friend, Jane Brabyn, who is the granddaughter of Sir Thomas Beecham and is herself a fine musician. She also has interesting and serious views about the conservation of old houses such as her own. Her policy is to repair when necessary, but not to renovate unduly, to allow the passage of time to show in the fabric of the buildings and to live with the character of her home, rather than trying to change it. Her sympathetic approach is one that conservationists are adopting in ever-increasing numbers in Great Britain and perhaps explains why this manor house

has such a tranquil atmosphere.

Designing dried flowers for such an individual home was a challenge. Rigid forms, overtly fashionable shapes and self-consciously clever designs were out. So were bright colours, which would have looked new and harsh. Nothing too simple was in order because these rooms are large and formal, yet neither was anything that was excessively smart or showy. Sometimes when you walk into a room it is immediately obvious what kind of arrangement is required. If it's not, I try to find inspiration from the fabrics, furniture and objects displayed in the room. Usually something will spark off an idea or a theme that I can use. In this case three things made an impression. First, the warm brown colours of the wooden floor and the bookcase. Second, the mosaic of colours and patterns in the rugs. And third, the colours and textures of the velvet curtains (not, sadly, visible in the picture) and the upholstery of the chair.

For the rug-draped ottoman we chose a large, traditional basket arrangement composed of clear, harmonious reds, yellows and oranges to give a warm but not too vivid

One classic arrangement and one
work of imagination, both
inspired by the colours, textiles
and patterns of this lovely room
and both successful on their own
terms

effect. The colour comes predominently from red and yellow roses and orange verticordia, but a closer look will reveal that it is studded with other colours. Pink heather, white gypsophila, blue hydrangeas and pale blue delphiniums and larkspur are just a few of the varieties mingled in with the green ferns. The effect is rather like that of the rugs, which are full of colours that one doesn't notice at first glance.

On the table by the windowsill we made a very free arrangement which is based round the extraordinary colours and textures of celosia, which looks like crushed velvet. In feel and appearance it is quite unlike any other kind of dried flower. I am normally fairly careful about the way I use this plant because there can be something almost too rich and opulent about it. In small quantities it is extremely useful for adding depth of colour and textural contrast to an arrangement, and it goes well in traditionally-styled Victorian settings full of velvet and moquette. It works here, I think, because it is tempered by the plainness of the surrounding foliage and the lack of pattern and strong colour in its immediate vicinity.

This is the kind of imaginative arrangement for which there are few guidelines. In fact almost the only thing I can recommend to those embarking on something totally original, like this, is to make it bold and not to stint

The strong shape and overwhelming darkness of this grand piano demands an arrangement with plenty of character – supplied here by a carved wooden statue surrounded by a thicket of wild-looking flowers and foliage. To the right of it, in complete contrast, is the only traditional triangular-shaped arrangement you'll find in this book. It's pretty, and still popular with people who like their flowers neat and tidy.

on materials. Apart from that, one simply has to trust one's own judgement. Personally, I believe it's worked here, and so did Jane Brabyn, who was appreciative of its free and full shape and liked the fact that it was so different from other, less creative, arrangements.

When it came to arrangements for the main hall of the manor with its huge stone fireplace and grand piano, it took us some time to work out what was needed. The piano is a wonderful feature, but because of its size and colour it tends to dominate the picture. Something was required to go on top of it, but a basket arrangement just wouldn't do. We needed something with more height and impact – but what? When, after some time, we'd come up with neither a container we felt was right for the setting, nor any ideas for an arrangement, we decided to try a different approach. We chose an object that had the right kind of height and impact, and decorated that.

If you ever find yourself in a similar state of creative paralysis, you might find this a useful way of freeing yourself. Forget your hidebound ideas of what makes a traditional arrangement and look around for other sources of inspiration.

One idea was sparked off by the number of musical instruments around the house. Many of them belong to Jane's partner Michael Tubbs, who is Music Director of the Royal Shakespeare Company and a brilliant musician. We contemplated making an arrangement incorporating a violin and bow, a flute, a roll of musical manuscript and any other musical bits and pieces we could gather. What we had in mind was a very stylized arrangement alluding to the woodcarvings of Grinling Gibbons, many of which included flowers. The idea had to be abandoned when we discovered that no one would lend us their precious flutes and violins, but it is something that I'd like to try in future.

A second suggestion was to use a classically shaped candelabra and add flowers to that. This was rejected, however, because it seemed rather clichéd, but I'm sure it would have looked good.

Our eventual solution was to base the arrangement around a wooden figure we have at Armscote. This is a carving of the Wandering Jew, Ahasuerus by name, which I bought at an auction some years ago. I remember the occasion particularly well because it was just after Fred and I were married and I'd gone to London with the intention of buying some furniture for our first home. I returned to the Cotswolds with nothing to show for the trip except the wooden statue. Fred was not impressed. I'm delighted, however, that after all this time my purchase has proved itself so useful!

The flowers had to be dramatic to stand out against the large scale of the piano and also to match the strong (some have even said malevolent) character of Ahasuerus. We developed a dense mass of multi-textured and coloured foliage from which the figure emerges. A branch cut from a smoke tree and preserved in glycerine provides the vertical element of a tall, curved shape that exploits the turning movement of the figure. Twigs covered in silver lichen, pink titree, tall sprays of yellow kangaroo paw and spiky grey-topped *Phylica rigida* give way to weeping pear, mahonia, ferns and beech arranged in a tightly-packed bunch. At the rear of the arrangement twisted banana branches add to the drama, suggesting the broken and twisted roots of an old tree. Glycerined ivy trails over the statue's arm and down on to the piano. Further strands tumble over the edges. The finishing touch is a bird's nest complete with eggs, half-hidden amidst the foliage and positioned so that it's the focus of Ahasuerus' wild gaze. This is not a traditionally 'pretty' arrangement, but a strong, dramatic creation that reflects its setting.

*The two splendid ducks, the wildlife embroideries standing behind them
and the watercolour on the wall behind the arrangement were our
inspiration for this moss-covered riverbank design. Children in
particular love this type of arrangement as they can keep adding things
to the miniature landscape.*

This is a good point at which to add a few words about the use of dried flowers on pianos. Vases of fresh flowers are usually banned from pianos because of the potential water damage to the wood and, disaster, the inner workings. With dried flowers there is no such danger. Furthermore, depending, of course, on the container, dried arrangements also have the advantage of being lighter than water-filled ones. This makes them particularly suitable for old and delicate pieces of furniture, radiator screens and for high shelves, where it would be difficult to keep lifting a heavy fresh arrangement up and down. I don't particularly wish to promote dried flowers for their practical advantages – they should stand by their looks alone – but they can, without doubt, be very useful additions to the interior design repertoire.

On now to two arrangements designed specifically to suit a particular item of furniture. The first, pictured on page 43, is a chest of drawers. When we saw the setting, with the ducks and the watercolours hanging on the wall, nothing came immediately to mind. We considered making a garlanded basket filled with pomanders, or a large, low basket full of russet-coloured flowers, but neither seemed entirely suitable. A glass bowl lined with moss and filled with pine cones, acorns, seed heads and flowers was more appealing, except that a plain glass bowl didn't seem to be totally in keeping with the setting. We at last realized that the work had already been done for us by the owner of the house. Our keys were the ducks and the watercolours depicting a peaceful country scene.

An arrangement fills the difficult gap left above a wardrobe perfectly. The shape, size and contents of the design were all planned and sketched beforehand so that we could judge the proportions.

The resulting arrangement is based on the idea of a riverbank. We filled a basket with off cuts of dry foam and covered it in different mosses – mounded green bun moss to create smooth rounded shapes, touches of lichen and greyish Spanish moss around the sides for texture and colour. We then looked for a variety of other materials that would be appropriate in this miniature landscape. Caustus, glycerined ivy, dried fungi, spiky skeletal agapanthus heads and small bell-shaped eucalyptus seeds were all wired into position. Interesting stones were brought in from the garden and glued into the arrangement. The final touches were the six bulrushes pushed firmly into the moss at the back.

A miniature landscape like this can be great fun, especially for children who love to keep adding things. I think you have to treat this kind of arrangement with a little humour, but because in this case the whole context – the slightly whimsical ducks (particularly the one on the left, which has a very peculiar look in its eye), the embroidery and the painting – was right, the arrangement fitted perfectly.

Our second design or 'set piece' was for the top of a wonderful old painted wardrobe, shown opposite, that formed a major feature in a spacious drawing-room. The problem with even the most beautiful wardrobes is that they tend to stop abruptly a foot or two from the ceiling, leaving a difficult and not always very attractive space. The owner of this particular piece of furniture often uses fresh material to fill the gap, but one can imagine the inconvenience of climbing up there with water-filled containers. Dried flowers were the obvious alternative.

Taking as a source of inspiration the nuts and flowers painted on the wardrobe itself, our first thought was to create an arrangement using oak leaves and acorns, nuts, fir cones and red flowers to add a touch of bright colour. By the time we had gathered a swatch of colours and materials, however, we realized that this was going to look too heavy and dark. Something lighter, both in texture and colour, was required. We began again with a new swatch and chose strong, sunny yellows as our main shade. When it came to selecting materials we looked for those with a strong, distinctive form that could be appreciated from ground level. The use of intricate textures and details is marvellous if they can be seen, but in an arrangement such as this, the detail would be lost so it is best to stick with strong simple forms.

Our final selection included the drumstick-shaped flowers of craspedia, kangaroo paw and yellow roses. Those invaluable fillers, carthamus, alchemilla and amaranthus supplied most of the greenery, while dark brown bracken gave the whole arrangement depth and solidity. Tucked in amongst the other material to give an occasional touch of more complex colour were a few rust-brown and orange flowers. Do try this yourself when you are making arrangements that are predominantly one shade. Just a few flowers of a different colour added so unobtrusively that the eye doesn't consciously see them can bring the whole arrangement to life.

Our materials were arranged in a low, mounded shape that trailed over the edge of the wardrobe. This was done purposely to break-up the heavy top line of the piece. Without the fronds of bracken and kangaroo paw intruding over the edge, it would have looked as if our flowers were just sitting on the top – a decorative afterthought, but not an integral part of the picture.

I find it very useful when designing an arrangement like this to use a pencil and paper to sketch the setting and see how the design will look in context. Measure all the relevant fittings and items of furniture so that you can work out how tall or broad the arrangement needs to be.

Upstairs, now, to two bedrooms that couldn't be more different in design and atmosphere. While we were looking for our locations and planning the arrangements, we discussed the kind of dried flowers we had encountered in bedrooms in the past and were astonished to discover that everyone seemed to have a horror story to tell – of hotel bedrooms with bunches of pampas grass shedding all over the carpet, of elderly aunts whose spare rooms housed hideous, dusty bulrushes, and holiday apartments with sparse, fluff-covered arrangements of statice beside each bed. It was a salutory experience.

Pampas grass and bulrushes certainly don't feature in our bedrooms, but I readily accept the point about dust. All dried flowers require occasional dusting, but it is particularly important in the bedroom, especially if one has an arrangement by the bed. Dust them regularly, using a large, soft paintbrush or a hair dryer on a low setting. One can also obtain a miniature vacuum device sold for cleaning computer keyboards and other inaccessible crevices. If you're using one of these, try it out at the back of the arrangement first, just in case it removes the flowers along with the dust.

Our first bedroom, shown on page 47, is traditionally pretty, decorated in soft colours and flowery fabrics. Something simple seemed in order and so we filled an attractively-shaped terracotta bowl with a low arrange-

Though this is a sophisticated bedroom, the exposed beams add a pleasing hint of rusticity. It's this contrast we wanted to echo in the bedside arrangement. A rustic terracotta bowl is complemented by a pretty, but pleasingly restrained, garden arrangement of roses, nigella and alchemilla. And surrounding it is a terracotta dish filled with potpourri.

ment of pink and crimson flowers. They include helichrysums, alchemilla, pink and white larkspur, roses, crimson-dyed quaking grass and nigella. The result is attractive enough to stand on its own, but we wanted to make it a little more special. Two ideas came to mind. One was to put the bowl in a larger terracotta saucer and fill the gap around it with more dried flowers. In the end, though, we decided to place the bowl at an angle to show off the flowers better, and filled the saucer with potpourri and pieces of broken pottery.

Potpourri is one of the oldest and most delightful ways of scenting a room and has been used in country houses since the Middle Ages. Used as part of an arrangement like this, it is pleasing to both the nose and the eye. We chose to use a traditional rose-based mixture to complement the flowers in the arrangement, but there are many other types of scent and mood to choose from. For something deeper and more spicy, try one based on heather or lavender with cinnamon and cloves. Citrus potpourri, containing dried orange and lemon peel, is tangy and refreshing, good for bathrooms, while for a man's dressing-room or study one might choose a mixture with overtones of cedar and sandalwood. One could even use potpourri as inspiration for a dried-flower arrangement. It would be fun, for example, to decorate a basket of spiced lavender mixture with a garland containing some lavender flowers, cinnamon sticks and pomanders stuck with cloves.

For the dressing-table, outlined against the mullioned stone window, we chose three small arrangements. On the left is a tree covered in the same combination of flowers we used in the bedside arrangement. If one is making a variety of arrangements for the same room it is generally wise to include some of the same materials in the arrangements, thus creating a link and a sense of continuity. This doesn't mean that the same flowers *have* to be used throughout. An occasional colour or textural contrast throws a new perspective on all the arrangements and can make them even more interesting.

Making a small tree like the one on the dressing-table is a relatively easy task. Instructions for setting the trunk in plaster are on page 69. A dry foam shape can be attached to the trunk once it has firmly set. Spheres and cones are commercially available from florists (see page 135) or you can carve your own irregular shape from a larger block. The next stage is to decide the effect you're aiming for and to choose your flowers accordingly. Celosia, used on its own, gives a wonderfully rich, velvety result. Helichrysums stuck densely all over can give a very full, mop-headed, effect. A plain green moss tree looks marvellously simple, particularly if it has an interesting, gnarled trunk. Alternatively if you cover a cone with dark green spikes of kunzea then you have a Christmas tree. Arrange a number of twigs together in the plaster and top them with greenery and you have a bonsai-sized copse. The possibilities are simply endless, limited only by the imagination.

In our case, we wrapped the tree's trunk in larkspur stalks to give it a more interesting texture and followed the contours of the sphere fairly closely when adding the flowers. The whole arrangement is finished off with bun moss piled around the base.

Next to it is a very simple, lace-edged posy, made to a formal design in a commercially available posy holder (see page 134). To the right, echoing the contents of the bedside arrangement, is a small basket of potpourri finished with a garland, another fragrant touch to a very feminine corner of the room.

There's not a posy or rosebud to be seen in our second bedroom pictured on pages 50-51. Situated in the attic of a

*For this traditionally pretty bedroom we chose small, neat arrangements.
The tree, posy and garlanded basket full of potpourri are ideal
attractive but unobtrusive additions to the dressing-table displaying
family photos.*

A fantasy bedroom. The sparse, romantic feel of the room is reflected in the arrangements. In the foreground, contorted willow branches create dramatic, visually exciting shapes. At the back, a bundle of reeds tied in a basic sheaf makes the simplest and least fussy of arrangements.

relied on architectural rather than decorative impact.

Back at Armscote we began to collect materials and colour samples, and found ourselves reaching automatically for light, cool colours – blues, greys, whites, silvers – and materials with an airy feel or strong form. It was a disconcerting experience. Where were the reds and oranges normally used to provide warmth? Where were the bunches of green foliage to act as fillers? We understood instinctively that we wanted to do something different, but avoiding established ways of thinking proved difficult at times.

The material that really inspired us and provided the key for the other arrangements was a bundle of contorted willow bought from New Covent Garden market in London (see page 135). This is wonderful stuff, with branches that naturally twist into tortured shapes. It is often cut, stripped of its leaves and added to flower arrangements to give instant movement and drama. As soon as we snipped the strings that bound our bundle together and watched the branches splay out into their contorted, windblown shapes, we knew we had our first arrangement. The willow was fixed in an old churn and finished with a bunch of silvery-white seacrest. The result was scarcely typical country house style, but was exactly suited to its location.

The other large arrangement standing against the back wall is equally simple and yet it was a real discovery. We came across it by accident during a trip to the Royal Show at Stoneleigh in Warwickshire, where almost every facet of farming and country life is represented in displays, competitions and exhibits. Among those demonstrating their country crafts were a group of thatchers who, as well as explaining the finer points of their art, showed us samples of the different reeds that were available to them. We came away with a bundle of the longest

fascinating old house that stands on its own in a gloriously rolling Cotswold valley not far from Northleach, it's a fantasy creation – a room for a romantic individualist with a strongly dramatic streak. The house itself is a mysterious place, the remaining wing of what must once have been a country residence built on a grand and imposing scale. It's said to be haunted by two ghosts, one of whom makes occasional appearances in the attic. I have to report that we saw nothing of it while we were there, but the atmosphere of the place certainly influenced our choice of arrangements.

The sparse, fantastic feel of the room was perplexing at first after the comfortable, colourful interiors we were used to. What kind of arrangements could adequately reflect the attic's character? Country baskets and traditionally pretty garlands were out. They were too sturdy, too solid and, anyway, not large enough to make much impact. What was needed in this environment were designs with an ethereal quality; sparse, fantastical arrangements that reeds they had, tied them into a sheaf, and for less than two pounds achieved an arrangement of extraordinary simplicity and dramatic impact.

In a romantic gesture we cast practicality to the wind and hung a swing from the central roof beam. As the heavy nylon ropes were rather less romantic than desired, we covered them in grey Spanish moss, which was then trimmed with delphiniums, white *Helichrysum vestitum capblumen*, known as vestitum, and blue-dyed glixia. For the pelmet across the doorway and the curtain tie-back we used a narrow garland wired with sea lavender, gypsophila, dark blue delphiniums and statice, glixia and more of the white daisies. Informal bunches of statice and delphiniums, with alchemilla, poppy heads, bleached grasses and nigella added extra colour and texture tucked into an enamel jug and hung from the bedpost. Behind the bed an old tin hatbox was filled with spiky delphiniums and white larkspur, with the button-shaped heads of botao and sprays of oats and sea lavender. The overall effect is almost surreal. It's a place of the imagination, of fantasy – perhaps even of ghosts.

One wouldn't normally put flowers on a sunny windowsill because the light makes them fade quickly, but as this was a fantasy room free from the constraints of practicality we chose to bend the rules. We found an old fireplace fender that matched the size of the heavy beam running under the window and filled it with a long row of flowers. The same materials were used as elsewhere in the room, with the botao 'buttons' providing a central focal point. Our search for materials turned up an anonymous bundle of fine, wispy reeds, which we inserted in clumps to give the arrangement height and found they added a rather mysterious feel. The lower, stubbier clumps are bunches of glixia stems, cut off when the glixia were wired and re-used here. There can be a great deal of wastage in dried-

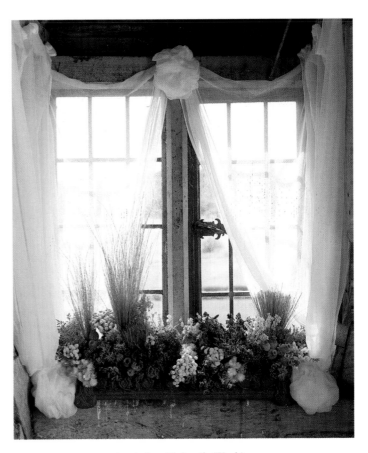

A windowsill detail. Working with sharp, 'difficult' colours can be a rewarding experience. Too often we play safe with pretty, inoffensive colours that give us bland results. As long as an arrangement works in context, as this one does, it really doesn't matter whether it's pretty or not.

flower arranging, especially if one is wiring-up small bunches of flowers to insert in larger arrangements for a pleasingly full effect. I like to find interesting ways of recycling some of the discarded stalks and foliage, as here, for example, or to cover baskets or miniature tree trunks.

Our interest in dramatic form and shape inspired one last arrangement, which we used to top a makeshift bookcase constructed from an old stepladder. The overall height and shape was provided by silver tentacles of seacrest, this time juxtaposed with the wonderful spiky shapes of globe thistles. All the materials were arranged in a tall glass tank lined with silver-blue lavender potpourri.

This lining technique is not difficult but can take time to achieve a pleasing result. Start by measuring the dimensions of the container and cutting a piece of dry foam to go inside, leaving a gap of between a quarter and half an inch (0.6-1.2cm) all round. Pour some of the lining material into the bottom of the container, insert the foam and hold in position while you pour lavender or potpourri

around it. If you have someone available to help, ask them to hold the foam and container. You can then try rolling-up a sheet of paper to make a narrow funnel and pouring the lavender through this, directly into position. The results vary dramatically according to the material you use for the lining. A rose-based potpourri gives a very dark, rich texture. Lavender is glistening and cool whilst cinnamon sticks poked down between the glass and foam give a stripy, woody texture. Different types of moss and lichen, used together or separately, create a variety of patterns.

Too often people's conception of dried flowers is limited to basket arrangements and vases filled with dusty, long dead material. But that very same material can become high art when used with a little imagination. What I hope we've demonstrated in this attic is that dried flowers can be as dramatic and as visually exciting as you dare to make them. Whatever the mood or effect you want to achieve in your home, there are dried materials and techniques that can realize your vision.

An exercise in form, with tentacles of seacrest making a wonderful contrast to the prickly spheres of the globe thistles. Too often, as flower arrangers, we wire and trim our material into the shapes we require for traditional, unimaginative arrangements. It's a liberation, once in a while, to look at the same material from a new perspective; to see not just its colour but its natural shape and form, and to use those natural qualities in an arrangement.

TOWN MEETS COUNTRY

Traditional manor houses like those featured in this book, most of them built in the sixteenth and seventeenth centuries, have a special charm that appeals to people the world over. They are, for many, the classic embodiment of the smaller English country house. But it would be a mistake to forget all the other beautiful houses of later centuries – particularly those Georgian and early Victorian houses that make such wonderful country homes. The style and character of such houses is quite different from the old manors. Later architecture followed new lines that were a self-conscious move away from the low ceilings and dim interiors of the older houses. If traditional manors were characterized by the huge stone hearths and wooden beams dominating their rooms, those houses of the eighteenth and nineteenth centuries offered large windows, high ceilings and detailed decoration.

The change in style was influenced not just by architectural fashion, but by a deeper social change that drew people away from the country to live in the city. The poor went to cities to find work. The rich went to enjoy themselves. (Anyone who is familiar with the novels of Jane Austen will remember how many of her characters longed to escape from the boredom of the countryside for the bright lights and adventure of Bath and London.) A landowner visiting his country estate wanted a house in which he could enjoy some of the comforts and sophistications he'd learned to appreciate in town. And so we get beautiful Georgian and, later, Victorian houses – houses that bring a touch of the city to the countryside.

When we visited houses like this, we realized that our dried-flower arrangements would need to reflect their sophisticated character without becoming too formal. Our first challenge was the vast, soft-white painted reception-room pictured on page 57 with its impressive marble fireplace and detailed plasterwork panels, typical of many a town house. The room could have been very grand, but instead it has been furnished with sofas and chairs in traditional chintzes that give it a comfortable and lived-in feel. The white walls and plain wooden floor, scattered with old rugs, have a clean, modern look. We decided to combine the two, modern and traditional, for a series of arrangements on the mantlepiece.

The clear, pretty colours of the chintz set the colours of our arrangements, and for containers we chose a variety of styles, new and old. We began with the new. Two tall glass vases were lined with a mixture of lavender and rose petals and filled with rich, unashamedly pretty arrangements of pink roses, larkspur and titree, with green amaranthus and the spidery seed heads of *Nigella orientalis,* a new and very attractive introduction. Touches of strong blue-green glixia added a note of contrast – a necessity if the arrangements weren't to look too cloyingly pretty. The tops of the vases were covered with plaited paper ribbon for a neat and distinctive look.

For the other arrangements we used some of the owner's cachepots and filled each of them with different combinations of flowers in the same colour theme. To the one on the left were added bright pink clumps of silene,

Variations on a theme inspired by chintz. New glass vases and old porcelain cachepots make compatible companions on this imposing mantelpiece. When you are grouping arrangements together like this, use an uneven number. Three or five arrangements always look better than two or four.

soft yellow verticordia, apricot-coloured statice, hydrangeas, dyed gypsophila, helichrysums and wonderfully full-blown peonies. The pot in the centre is packed with small bunches of different coloured glixia, which together give a dappled light-and-shade effect. On the right-hand side there are more roses and *Nigella orientalis*, arranged with botao heads and the tiny bead-like heads of flax. Glixia and alchemilla add areas of sharper colour. Five arrangements on a single mantelpiece may seem extravagant, but the best way of using dried flowers for a really bold statement is to do so lavishly. Incidentally, when grouping arrangements together always use an odd number, never even. For some reason an odd number of items, whatever they are, always looks better than two, or four or other even combinations.

In the fireplace below is the kind of arrangement that everyone with an open fire should have. It's by far the most attractive way of filling a hearth in the summer months, when blazing log fires are out of fashion. No more yawning black holes in the wall or unseasonal piles of pine cones thrown hastily into the grate. Suddenly, the fireplace becomes the focal point of the room, as it is supposed to be. The peonies are particularly spectacular in this arrangement. Their large, distinctively-textured flowers really stand out from this angle. It's helpful when you're making an arrangement that will go on the floor, like this one, to put it down occasionally and check it from the angle at which it will be viewed. Insert the strongest, most dramatic flowers and materials where they will have the maximum impact – which is not necessarily where you would imagine it to be if you are working on a table.

To achieve the required height and span in this kind of arrangement, fill the top of the container with scrunched chicken wire pulled roughly into the shape you're aiming for – in this case a tall mound, flat at the back and sloping gradually down at the front. There's something of a mystique about using chicken wire, and it's quite unfounded. Most people find that once they have mastered the skill they prefer it to dry foam. To start, take a piece of one and a half inch (3cm) gauge wire (see page 134), that's six inches (15cm) or so bigger all round than the top of the container – allow for more if it's particularly large or if you want to make a shape that rises above it. Taking each edge in turn, loosely tuck them under by two or three inches (5-7.5cm). Do this once more and then fit the resulting mass of wire into the container. It should fit firmly. If it feels loose, remove it and pull it out a little. Fix it in place with wires threaded through the basket weave or with florists' tape (see page 134). Now all you have to do is cut the flowers to length and push them into place. If the chicken wire has been properly prepared the various layers will catch the stems and hold them securely. It's a technique suitable for most types of containers and all sorts of arrangements. The three cachepots on the mantelpiece, for example, were all arranged with chicken wire.

Chicken wire is the underpinning, too, of the beautiful wall wreath featured opposite. When we first discussed ideas for some kind of arrangement to go on the wall, we had dim memories of flowery ceramic wall plaques of the 1920s and 30s. Their strong relief and irregular gaps and contours were our initial inspiration, though the finished article bears little resemblance to the original – which is as it should be. Concrete references and ideas should be the springboards for inspiration, nothing more.

For the basic shape of our dried-flower wall plaque we used a child's plastic hula-hoop and covered it in thick layers of moss and chicken wire to create a flat, irregular wreath. Two thick twigs were placed across the gap, mossed and wired into place. The basic structure com-

*Wall flowers. Wreath arrangements offer really creative opportunities if
you don't limit yourself to symmetrical shapes and designs. Make your
own irregular bases and experiment with colour in your arrangement,
starting with light shades and progressing to the darkest you can find.
Use flowers for painterly effects, as shown here, or play with texture in
a dramatic way. See, for example, how effectively button-shaped botao
heads have been grouped to create a strong, suede-textured area.*

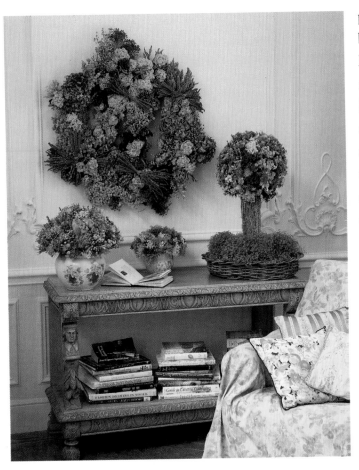

A small tree takes up the chintz theme, its pot embedded in a basket of mind-your-own-business plants (Soleirolia soleirolii). On the wall beside it a wonderfully textured and coloured wreath shows off massed salmon pink roses and the delicate frilled petals of peonies.

plete, the background material – alchemilla, dyed broom bloom, yellow verticordia, flax, amaranthus and pink larkspur – was added. Over this background went the roses, peonies, hydrangeas, lavender bunches and botao buttons, all arranged in strong groups of concentrated colour and texture that made a real feature of their individual qualities. To open the roses and show them at their best, each was gently steamed over a kettle for a few seconds until it softened enough for its petals to be teased apart. The peonies were steamed and opened in the same way. The result of all this attention was an arrangement quite unlike anything seen before, a truly original design, full of beautiful flowers.

The Indian feel of the inlaid chest of drawers, shown on page 61, inspired another highly original design. We wanted to exploit the Indian theme and so as a starting point we made a list of the associations India has for us: these included rice, cotton, coconuts, cinnamon and a range of other more exotic spices. We then began collecting these and other materials that could be useful, not limiting ourselves too strictly to Indian plants and produce. A trip to the delicatessen produced licorice sticks, almonds, tamarinds in their brown, warty pods, knobbly pieces of dried root ginger and dried tomatoes. The brown and cream colour scheme, echoing that of the chest itself, was already beginning to emerge.

Elsewhere we gathered lotus seed pods, exotic-- looking seed heads, dark spires of dock, 'brown eyes' daisies, poppadums, nutmegs, bamboo sticks, vanilla pods. Attempts to find dried cotton, rice and even tea failed, but by then we had enough material for our arrangement. The result, as you can see, is dramatically original and works well with the chest of drawers that inspired it. On a purely practical note, when you're using fruit, nuts or anything that might leak or become sticky (the coconuts, for

An Indian-inspired arrangement, witty and sophisticated, packed with intriguing and unusual contents, including lotus pods, poppadums, nutmegs, bamboo sticks and vanilla pods. It is dramatically original and perfect for its setting.

example) in an arrangement, line the container with plastic so that no damage is done to the furniture.

Of course there are many other types of arrangement that could have worked well in this position. A simple basket filled with flowers in shades of yellow, brown and green would have looked pleasing, though perhaps rather dull. On a more adventurous note, an arrangement with mother-of-pearl shells, like those used for the chest inlay, could have been visually exciting – although perhaps a little gaudy for this calm setting. Maybe, taking into account the seascape on the wall, an arrangement based on an interesting piece of driftwood would have been appropriate. Not all settings inspire this number of options, but by simply looking for associations one is usually agreeably surprised by the ideas that emerge.

Another bold arrangement in its use of exotic material, shown opposite, was created for a difficult corner of a living-room. It was difficult because of the busy background of the quilt and the strong shape of the painted wooden horse that was already standing in front of it. Despite the fact that both horse and quilt have a rustic look, together they create a sophisticated visual combination. Any arrangement that was to complement them had to be equally commanding. A country basket simply wasn't going to be enough.

As starting points we took the strong brown and red colours in the horse's saddle and the spiky triangular motifs of the quilt. Fortunately the ideal container, a red and black water carrier bought on a holiday in Thailand, was soon found and the search for materials began. Spiky palm spears and the strongly serrated leaves and bristly heads of *Banksia baxteri* were obvious choices for their form. Vibrant red verticordia and celosia, brown-dyed broom bloom and reddish-brown capucin leaves joined the pile. So did the grey, fluffy textures of *Phylica rigida*,

dark red helichrysums, proteas, some dramatic brown seed pods and the cream-coloured spikes of dryandra. Dusty, blue-black, preserved palm berries were piled into the lid of the water carrier, which was set down in front of the arrangement. The result was about as far from a traditional country house style as one could possibly get, wildly exotic, highly dramatic, and absolutely right for this particular location.

There is a kind of flair and boldness about this arrangement which I associate with the European school of floristry. The Dutch and Germans lead the way in continental flower design, and their ideas and arrangements are often strikingly different from English style. So many English florists and gardeners, myself included, love the idea of informality, wildflowers, cottage gardens, simple arrangements – in short, the natural look. The Dutch and Germans do not share our near-obsession with nature. They love bright, dyed colours, artificial shapes and exotic material used in fantastic ways – a kind of floral modernism that leaves most English observers in a state of shock.

I have an example of this type of modern, continental arrangement at Armscote and sometimes use it to surprise visitors who ask me about fashions in dried flowers. It was made for me by a wonderful young Dutch designer who came to Armscote two or three years ago to help develop

Exotic flowers and spiky textures mingle in this bold, brave arrangement with more than a dash of continental flair. Fearful English florists might quail at the thought of grouping banksias, palm spears and proteas in front of this rustic-looking setting, but a touch of drama is exactly what the grouping requires. It's a lesson to all of us, myself, I admit, included, in how to use exotic materials with style.

some new ideas for our range. At the end of her time with us, during which she produced lots of wonderful arrangements, I suggested she let herself go and make something more creative in her own favourite style. The result was a white plastic bowl filled with metallic florentine branches, corn cobs, gypsophila and glixia, much of it sprayed with pale green metallic paint. Bleached *Briza segromi*, she told us, represented the female and the corn cobs the male – and we had no problem at all in understanding the symbolism. When I show it to English guests and ask their opinion there is a silence followed by a gulp and a strangled, 'Well, it's . . . interesting.' Not a very flattering response.

It's not, fortunately, difficult to find something flattering to say about the pair of daisy trees that flank the garden door in the picture on the right. In season a pair of real daisy trees occupy this position, but at other times of the year these dried-flower lookalikes replace them. You need a large-scale setting and plenty of confidence to carry off arrangements this size, but if you have both then the effect can be quite spectacular. Large trees are at their best when they are used symmetrically in pairs (this is the one exception to the odd numbers rule cited on page 58), as they are here. They'd look good standing either side of a fireplace or at the base of an imposing staircase.

When one is making a major statement with arrangements such as these, I would advise a fairly conservative choice of colours and materials. Bright, clashy shades are fun for small trees, but used in something larger and more attention-grabbing they may soon become tiresome. I'm rather keen on the 'fake' idea, which adds a touch of sophistication to the concept. A fake rose tree, covered in dark green moss and foliage and dotted with roses, could be fun. So might fake box trees, made of small-leaved foliage, or a moss-covered tree with dark hydrangea blooms. If you would like to make trees of your own, large

or small, there are full instructions on page 68.

Finally, to a very individual bathroom. Like kitchens, bathrooms aren't normally considered to be the best place for dried flowers. But there are bathrooms and bathrooms, and this one is not the small, steamy type and so it is a perfectly practical place to have dried flowers. Several small arrangements were made to dot around the room. On the left, in front of the bird cage, is a tree with two flowering heads. The flowers include roses, botao buttons, glixia, titree and carthamus, with the pink spikes of *Paranomus sphathulatus*.

Hanging from the dresser are three flower pomanders, all variations on the same colour theme. Pomanders like these are easy to make. Just take a commercially produced sphere of dry foam (if you can't find one in the right size you can carve your own from a larger block) and, resting it on a table, cover it with a selection of flowers keeping them packed tightly to prevent any gaps showing through. To finish the bottom, take a length of ribbon and a long, firm wire – if necessary, join two wires together. Bend the wire into a U-shape, then stick the ends through the ribbon and into the pomander, pushing them right through until they emerge at the bottom. Bend them upwards and back into the foam. This will hold the ribbon firmly in position. Hang the pomander up and finish covering it with flowers. Fragrance can be added with a few drops of essential oil applied either directly to the foam or to the flowers. Add more oil to refresh the pomander as and when it's needed.

An old chamber-pot forms the container for the main arrangement. The bathroom seemed an appropriate place

*Linking house and garden, a pair
of dried-flower daisy trees in
perfect counterpoint each side of a
well-framed door*

64

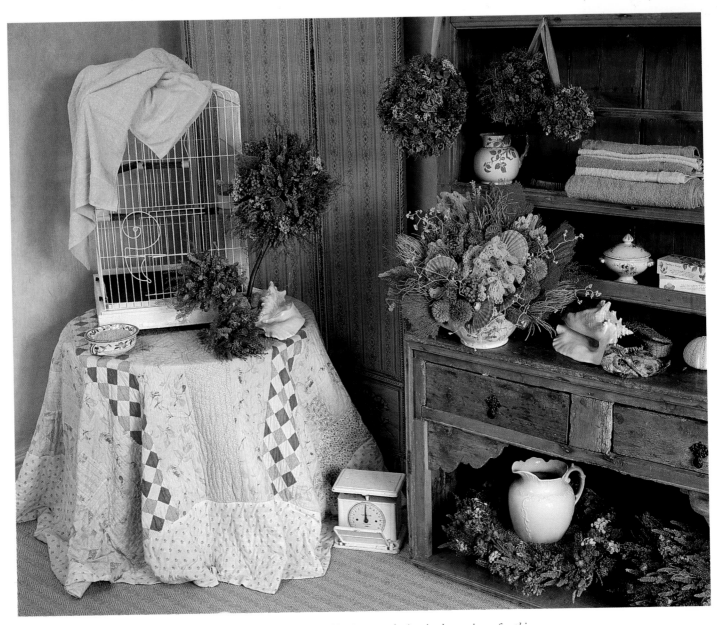

A chamber-pot and a jug and basin set make inspired containers for this
sophisticated bathroom. Sponges and loofah-type material are the
starting point for the main arrangement, while fragrance is supplied by
the perfumed pomanders and the lavender-filled basin.

for a display of flowers with a watery theme, centred on sponges against a background of coral fans, shells (contributed from her collection by my daughter, Sophie) and assorted bits of loofah-type material. Echoing the prickly textures are globe thistles, banksia heads and caustus, while pink-dyed botao heads add bright patches of colour that hold the arrangement together. All of our sponges and materials came from a specialist supplier, but one could just as easily use the kind of natural sponges and loofahs commercially available in most chemists' and drug stores.

While we were working out what kind of accessories to use for this bathroom photograph, our stylist brought out an attractive basin and jug set, which were instantly seized upon and taken to the work-room. There a mossed garland was attached to the rim using florists' tape (see page 134) on the delicate porcelain, and small bunches of roses, carthamus, amaranthus and lavender were wired into place. The bowl was filled with lavender and the jug placed in it. Once again we had a successful and surprise arrangement inspired by an unusual container.

I've mentioned the importance of containers elsewhere in this book, but it is worth repeating. Whatever it is – a porcelain jug sitting empty in a bedroom, an old wooden box used for storing toys, a junk-shop bargain you never quite knew what to do with – the right container will be the inspiration for something brilliantly original. When you're stuck for ideas for a special arrangement, don't just reach for a vase or a basket. Search the house and garden, climb up to the attic, excavate the junk cupboard for that one elusive and inspirational item that's just waiting there to be discovered.

Making the Arrangement
A DAISY TREE

In the spring and summer months two real daisy trees flank this doorway. For autumn and winter, when the plants are not at their best, we made this pair of trees to take their place. By varying the material used for flowers and foliage it's possible to achieve a wide variety of styles – anything from an almost real bay tree or standard rose bush to abstract designs in unnatural colours. The choice of trunk is almost as important as the foliage. A gnarled old apple branch creates one effect, a straight, slim beech branch another. Even when you are making small trees with trunks perhaps only a few inches tall, look for a piece of branch with a good shape or interesting bark texture. If you cut a fresh branch for your tree allow it to dry out for two weeks before you use it. Otherwise it may shrink and come loose from the plaster base.

At Armscote I like to use terracotta pots for our decorative trees. Not only do they look good, but they give weight and solidity to the finished tree. After blocking any drainage holes with a piece of card, the pots are filled with a mixture of thistle plaster (or strong wall plaster) and ozone-friendly polystyrene packaging bubbles, a combination discovered only after long experimentation. When it sets, plaster generates heat that can crack the pot. Once set, it shrinks. The polystyrene bubbles solve both problems, expanding and contracting with the plaster and gripping firmly to the walls of the pot to create a stable base. To finish the pot I usually fill the top with a layer of moss held in place with a few spots of glue. For something a little different you could use potpourri or, for a really splendid feature, make a dried-flower garland and attach it round the rim of the pot.

Once you've gone to the trouble of making a dried-flower tree it's a simple matter to refresh it if it begins to fade or to adapt it to suit a new location. By replacing the flowers with new material you can create a new tree to suit any setting.

MATERIALS REQUIRED
- *A large pot*
- *Thistle plaster*
- *Expanded polystyrene packaging bubbles*
- *Branch*
- *Mixing bowl and water*
- *Dry foam blocks*
- *Narrow tape*
- *Glue*
- *Scissors and a knife*
- *Stub wires*
- *Lupidium, ambrosinia or similar feathery green dried foliage, helipterums or other daisy-like material and sphagnum moss*

1 Mix the thistle plaster to a smooth, creamy consistency with water. Add the expanded polystyrene packaging bubbles – a handful for a small pot, more for a larger one. Pour the plaster mixture into the container and place the branch in the centre. Prop in position until set and trim to the size required.

2 Attach blocks of dry foam firmly to the branches using narrow tape and, if necessary, glue. When placing the blocks, bear in mind the finished shape you want to achieve.

3 Add the base material. We used lupidium, which has stiff stems that are easily inserted into the foam. For a more dense, bunched effect or when using softer material, wire a number of stems together (see page 118) and stick the wires into the foam.

4 Bunches of helipterum were wired in clusters of varying shapes and sizes and inserted randomly amongst the foliage to create the daisy-tree effect. To finish off place a layer of moss around the base of the tree so that the plaster mixture is not visible.

CHAPTER THREE
OUTDOOR
PERSPECTIVE

According to the rules, dried flowers should not be used outdoors — but they make such a wonderful contrast to the natural materials found there, weathered stone, mellow brick and wood, that it would be a shame not to break the rules occasionally. I particularly like to use them for special celebrations, when their sheer impracticality adds to the sense of occasion.

Simple bunches and buckets of flowers in a rustic lean-to. Strictly speaking dried flowers should not be used outdoors — but having seen how good they look here, who could fail to be tempted?

EXTERIORS

Dried flowers outdoors? Dried flowers for decorating front doors, porches – a gazebo? Were we crazy?

There were several sceptical glances when I suggested that we include a chapter on exteriors in this book. 'But what if it rains?' everyone asked. I will be the first to admit that dried flowers are not the most practical way of decorating an exterior feature. Neither are fresh flowers. If practicality is everything, we should head straight for plastic fakes. But dried flowers can look wonderful outdoors for special occasions. And if one takes reasonable care and doesn't expect them to be a permanent fixture, then why not use them?

As the picture on the previous page shows, you don't have to design elaborate formal arrangements to achieve a very pleasing effect. We took this photograph in the delightfully ramshackle lean-to of a manor house only a few miles from Armscote. It's a working farm producing wonderful organic lamb, and its owner has no intention of turning it into a design showpiece. But when we used it to display a selection of dried and fresh flowers it was utterly transformed. There are no clever or wildly original arrangements here, just a few dried bunches hanging casually from a post, some old buckets containing a variety of dried vegetables and garden flowers and some fresh artichokes, peonies, eryngium, honesty and leek heads all hanging up to dry. But they're appropriate to the functional appearance of the lean-to and, without making it look too fussy or unnatural, quietly make it a more attractive feature of the house.

There's no point in being unrealistic about using dried flowers outside. They obviously survive best in dry, airy conditions and out of direct sunlight, which destroys their natural colour. Bunches and bucket arrangements left under the shelter of this lean-to for the summer would probably end up battered, bleached and, if it was a poor year, damp and perhaps rotten. But if one chooses tough and what I rather unflatteringly call 'expendable' materials, then this doesn't really matter. The plants I have in mind are those that grow abundantly in most gardens – achillea, helichrysums, sea lavender, statice, eryngium, nigella, catmint, marjoram – all flowers that are useful fillers for arrangements but are not highly-prized; flowers that might perhaps be left on the plant if you already had enough of them dried and in store. Save roses, delphiniums and the more delicate and rare material for indoor use, but cut and dry these less special plants for use outdoors. Wildflowers such as buttercups and cow parsley (also known rather more elegantly as Queen Anne's lace) can be found in hedgerows and untended land, and used in sheltered exterior spots throughout the summer. They can then be thrown away later in the year or, if they've survived the experience, added to interior arrangements.

This all rather takes it for granted that you will be drying your own flowers. It's not necessary to do so, of course. There are excellent suppliers of dried flowers to be found in most areas these days (see page 135). But if you have a garden, do try it. It's the kind of task, like embroidering cushion covers or making your own preserves, that isn't strictly necessary but does give a great sense of personal satisfaction.

If you don't have a garden then you can buy bunches of roses, cornflowers, peonies and larkspur in summer, when they are plentiful, and dry them at home. Or you could try asking friends and neighbours if you could cut an armful of alchemilla or nigella, or a few hydrangea heads from their garden. You might even consider an informal business arrangement with a keen local gardener, so that he grows a few flowers each year specially for you. The results will be worth it, I promise. Your own carefully dried and tended flowers will be in much better condition and have a fresher look than bought material. And, something I value when I use my own home-grown flowers, the arrangements you make from them will hold memories for you – of a visit to a friend's garden, a surprise bouquet, an afternoon spent gathering moss in the forest.

All fresh material, whatever its source, should be properly dried before it's used for arrangements anywhere, indoors or out. There are several different drying methods (see page 130 for further details) but the simplest and most common method used is air drying. This is the process we employ most widely at Armscote and is the easiest for using at home. Divide freshly-cut material into bunches of four or five stems (leave large flowers or seed heads – artichokes, for example – single) and secure with twine. Hang them upside down somewhere warm, dark and dry with plenty of circulating air (see page 130). When I first started the business at Armscote we dried tons of home-grown flowers in this way in one of the barns. Today we require such quantities that we are forced to buy them in from local and foreign sources, but we still dry some of the more delicate material on the premises. When both flowers and stalks have dried out, which can take anything from a week to over a month, the material is ready to be used. By adding a little heat to the circulating air this process can be speeded up, and I find the quality and colour of the flowers is improved.

Examples of the vast variety of materials that can be dried and the uses to which they can be put are illustrated in the more detailed picture of the lean-to overleaf. The contents of the bicycle basket displays some of the riches

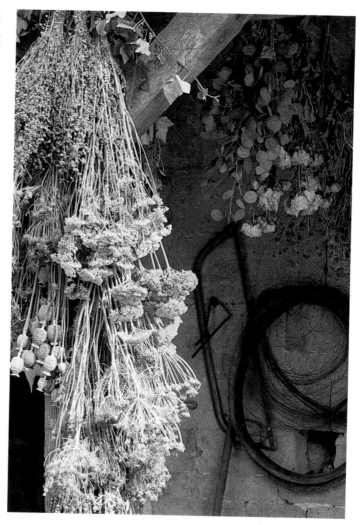

Sunlight, wind and rain are all natural enemies of dried flowers, and one can't expect dried materials used out of doors to last for long. But if you choose the toughest and most abundant varieties from your garden – achillea, eryngium and poppies, for example – and use them in a sheltered spot, it's possible to make an effective display that has a chance of withstanding the elements. Here the easiest of all arrangements, hanging bunches, help to transform a functional lean-to into an attractive feature of the house.

freely available in a well-planned garden. At the front is a bunch of green honesty. Honesty is so easy to grow and dry that its papery brown seed heads have become a terrible cliché in the flower-arranging world. This seems a pity because it can be very attractive, particularly at this stage when it has such a good colour. Dried carefully, in the dark, it should retain its greenness.

Next to it in the basket are the extraordinary conical seed heads of *Allium siculum,* a hardy bulb growing up to four feet high. In early summer it produces attractive white bell-shaped flowers which have tinges of green and purple. Once the blooms are over the seed heads can be cut for drying and make a strikingly structural contribution to arrangements. By the side of these are the bulbous seed heads of the beautiful orange and yellow Peruvian lily, alstroemeria, which makes a bold splash of colour in the garden throughout the summer. They are backed by fresh-cut green poppy heads which turn to silvery blue when dry.

The little basket on the wall is full of fresh flowers waiting to be prepared for drying. The gorgeous bright yellow-green of alchemilla, beloved of all flower arrangers, is an excellent foil to the dark, spiny stems of acanthus, which look very dramatic once dried. Tucked in with them are bunches of golden-yellow buttercups, which keep their colour well after drying, and shaggy-textured leek heads, perfect for large-scale arrangements.

Rich pickings from the garden. A bicycle basket is packed with freshly-picked seedheads while alchemilla, buttercups, peonies and leek heads wait to be dried. On the left is the Armscote Manor alternative windowbox, with flowers arranged by my husband Fred and daughter Sophie.

The bucket, at ground level, contains a prickly selection of maize and artichokes, both of which can be preserved by air drying. They'll take longer than most other materials to dry out, but the results are worth waiting for. In with them are silver-blue globe thistles and the large daisy-style flower heads of the carline thistle.

Above this, in an extremely battered wooden trough exhumed from one of the old greenhouses at Armscote, is a whimsical arrangement that looks quite at home in this rustic setting. I've mentioned the important part containers play in inspiring ideas previously, and this old box is yet another example of an unlikely container giving life to an unconventional but successful arrangement.

The idea was originally sparked off by someone who was looking for unusual windowboxes to photograph for a book. We couldn't help with a real windowbox, but the idea stayed with us and we made this one instead. Because we wanted to make something a little more interesting than a traditional windowbox, we filled the trough with terracotta pots of all shapes and sizes, old ones, new ones, broken ones – everything we could find around the garden. These were packed with moss and then Fred and Sophie spent a pleasant hour or two finishing them off with the most unlikely and colourful selection of odds and ends they could lay their hands on. One could, of course, have filled them with a more realistic selection of flowers and leaves, so that the box looked as if it was full of growing plants. I think our version is great fun, a family arrangement, packed with an eclectic combination of smoke bush, lavender, achillea, roses, globe amaranth, carthamus, buttercups, poppies . . . the list goes on. For anyone who has ever palled at the price of a large, eye-catching arrangement I offer this as an example of the kind of thing one can make almost for free.

One couldn't, alas, say the same of the dried flowers

used to dress the gazebo at Armscote for a spring party, shown opposite. It's lovely to have such an elegant feature in the garden and great fun to use it for a special occasion, particularly when we can make it look this good. Naturally we wouldn't have decorated it if the weather had been bad, but fate smiled on us; the day was fine and the garlands and pots survived not only the party but also the night, apparently quite unscathed by dew. I wouldn't recommend leaving them out for any longer than this without some form of protection, but I think dried material is considerably tougher and more tolerant than we imagine. If it does get wet, dry it immediately in warm, dark, airy conditions. As long as it hasn't been soaked through it should look relatively unscathed.

When it came to deciding on material for decorating an English country garden we couldn't think of anything better than roses and lavender which were incorporated freely into the arrangements. The basic designs were very simple, based on a background of dark green sparsa interspersed with lighter green caustus. This scheme was carried all the way through, with a few additions. To the large and relatively free arrangement at the back of the gazebo we added acanthus branches with some of their white flowers still attached. These almost imperceptible touches help to lighten the arrangement. It is important when you are working on an arrangement of this scale, particularly one that is not going to be seen from close quarters, to use your dried flowers as if they were paint, adding broad strokes and large splashes of colour, rather than diluting the effect with too much detail.

We used more of the acanthus, with its spiky, distinctive shape, in the stone pots in front of the gazebo. To these were added strong green eucalyptus leaves, which echoed the shape and colour of the bluebells in the flower-beds. The finished effect was quite magical, well worth the effort and admired by everyone who saw it. Hard work, maybe, but it turned a pleasant evening into something memorable.

It's almost a crime to intrude on the scene with thoughts about the practicality of using dried flowers like this, but that's inevitably the kind of question that springs to most people's minds. The good news is that something like this need not be wasteful or extravagant if one plans it so that the materials and arrangements can be re-used. All the flowers could have been taken down and stored until the next garden party, for example – try doing that with fresh flowers! Or if the next special occasion is too far off to merit storing them, they could be used indoors. Those beautiful stone pots could be taken straight in to stand each side of a hearth, or on a landing. The garlands, too, would make a spectacularly romantic feature in a bedroom or, with the roses quickly removed and holly and silver balls wired in place, a wonderful Christmas decoration for the hall or living-room. And the material from the back of the gazebo could be incorporated into a wide variety of arrangements – anything from a large and beautiful basket to a standard rose tree or two. There need, in fact, be no waste at all.

The gazebo at Armscote Manor decorated for a spring party. Treat arrangements like these as purely temporary exterior features and bring them into the house as soon as you can.

OUT OF DOORS

There are some occasions, of course, when extravagance is in order, and a wedding is one of them. It's difficult to think of a better way of welcoming the wedding party to the church than by decorating the entrance with flowers, and that's exactly what we did (see left) at St James the Great's, a tiny twelfth-century church in Idlicote, just up the road from Armscote. (To see how we coped with the interior turn to page 88.)

The garland arranged around the porch matches the one we used inside. It's a broad and very richly textured arrangement, full of brilliant red roses, hydrangeas, lilac achillea, statice, larkspur and celosia. The weather was good enough for us to pin it outside the porch on the day, but had it been raining or damp we would simply have moved it further inside and draped it around the door. Hung as it was, it made an excellent frame for the happy couple when they emerged after the service and posed for photographs.

In an unashamedly romantic gesture we hung a huge bow entirely covered in flowers on the church door. The top half was moulded from chicken wire and moss to make a flat pad, which was then studded with flowers. The hanging ties, covered in red-brown titree, were made from two lengths of mossed garland, with a flower-covered sphere

What better way to welcome guests to a wedding than with glorious flowers framing the church porch? A garland like this can be made well in advance and put up in just a few minutes. It creates an attractive backdrop for photographs after the service, and when the wedding is over it can be used to decorate the couple's home – a reminder of that very special day.

of dry foam at the end of each. A little over the top, perhaps, but all the more fun for that.

Of all the external features of a house, I think the front door is the most obvious and easy to decorate. So why not go ahead and do something with it? It's frivolous and unnecessary, true, but then so are many of the most satisfying things in life. A wreath or a garland on the front door is attractive and fun, a good way of greeting people as they arrive for a party or a special celebration. And when the party's over you can take down your exterior dried-flower arrangements and hang them up indoors.

The picture on page 80 shows the front door at Armscote Manor in summer splendour. In the four hundred years or thereabouts it has been here, I doubt whether it has ever looked quite so decorative. The garlands that hang each side of the door are full of mimosa and wonderfully exotic-looking lotus pods. At the bottom of each is a small oat sheaf, which echoes the larger sheaf pinned to the door itself. When the flowers are taken down they can be hung inside the hall, with the sheaf perhaps pinned to the back of the door.

Our front door is studded with ancient nails on which to hang such a sheaf or wreath, but if yours is not, and you don't want to damage it by hammering a pin into it then you can secure an arrangement by using fishing line and a drawing pin. Open the door wide and insert the tack or pin into the top edge, where a hole won't show. Press it down firmly, then try the door to ensure that it will still shut. (Most doors have sufficient gap at the top to allow this.) Cut a length of fishing line, loop it round the tack and bring it down the exterior of the door. Take the arrangement, thread the fishing-line through the wires at the back of it and secure it in the position required. The fishing line

ABOVE *The front door at Armscote Manor, decorated with garlands of mimosa, lotus seed heads and an oat sheaf. Frivolous, impractical, but a great way of welcoming guests to a party or marking a special occasion.* RIGHT *The freshest, most crisp arrangement in this book. Green Granny Smith apples set the tone for this spectacular double wreath decorated in sharp greens and white. We used the unusual double shape because we wanted an alternative to the traditional plain round wreath.*

will be almost invisible and the arrangement should hang safely, and without damaging the door.

Fishing line was not strong enough to support the last of our exterior arrangements photographed on page 81. It took a two-inch (5cm) nail to secure this apple-covered wreath, which contains at least six pounds of Granny Smith apples, to the door. It was the sharp colour of the apples that inspired the arrangement; the double-wreath shape developed because we were determined not to make an ordinary, single round one. Sometimes a stubborn refusal to do what's expected leads to very attractive results, as shown here. The top wreath is a crisp combination of colours that we would not normally think subtle enough to combine. White larkspur and helichrysums stand out boldly against the strong, clear greens of alchemilla, dyed glixia, white gypsophila and both standard and miniature varieties of honesty. The effect is brilliantly fresh and clean, positively mouthwatering.

The apples are simply pierced with wires and secured to a moss-covered wreath frame. They may last several weeks before drying out or beginning to rot. When this happens they can be removed and replaced, if desired, with a more durable material. Bunches of green-dyed or white botao buttons, or clumps of white helichrysums would also look striking against the dark green of the sphagnum moss.

Making the Arrangement
A ROPE GARLAND

Garlands are a wonderful way of decorating large areas of space and awkward places. You can wind them around banisters and handrails for a speedy transformation of the plainest staircase, spiral them around an old gazebo as we did, or drape them around doorways and picture frames. Wherever you use them their effect is always dramatic and extravagant.

The basic material needed to make a rope garland is, predictably enough, a rope. Use nylon rope as it is lighter and cheaper than other types. The diameter will influence the width of the finished garland, but for most purposes half an inch is suitable. The best way of finding the right length for your garland or swag is not to measure with a ruler or tape, but to drape the naked rope across the wall, down the staircase, round the gazebo, or wherever, and then cut it to size. For covering the rope you will need plenty of sphagnum moss. This can be bought from florists (see page 135) or you can gather it yourself. We collect some of the moss used at Armscote from a secret location in woods not far away, and its colour and texture are far better than the bought variety. It's best to use the freshly-gathered moss while it's still damp, as it is easier to handle, but let it dry out before adding the dried material.

In this demonstration you'll see how to make the garland we used for decorating the gazebo, but you can vary the contents as much as you like.

MATERIALS REQUIRED
- *Length of half-inch (1.2cm) nylon rope*
- *Reel wire and stub wires*
- *Scissors*
- *Sphagnum moss, fern, roses, caustus and lavender*

1 Bend a stub wire into a U-shape and attach it to the end of the rope with reel wire (see page 134) to make a loop from which the garland can be hung. Taking a handful of moss, bind it firmly around the rope with the reel wire. Add further clumps of moss, binding it in as you go with one continuous spiral of wire. Build up a thick layer that covers the rope completely. Add another hanging loop at the far end of the rope.

2 Take your basic material, in this case dried fern, and gather a few stems together to form a fan shape. Place this bunch at the end of the rope, covering the hanging loop, and bind it tightly with reel wire. Take the next bunch of fern, place it so that it slightly overlaps the first bunch and conceals the wires, and bind this in position also. Continue until the top of the whole rope is covered – don't bother with the underside, which will not be seen.

3 Make up small bunches of roses, caustus and lavender with stub wires. Allow a bunch of three roses for roughly every six inches of garland. Insert the roses at regular intervals along the garland, pushing the wires through the moss layer, out the other side and then threading the ends back into the moss.

4 Add the caustus and the lavender in the same way. Inspect the garland for visible wires and adjust the foliage and flowers to cover them. Hang the garland and check that the materials are evenly distributed. Adjust if necessary.

SPECIAL OCCASIONS

A winter wedding, a traditional Christmas celebration, a harvest or thanksgiving supper are just a few of the occasions when one is justified in going over the top with dried flowers. Used generously, they add a touch of magic and fantasy to any scene. And they're not just a spectacularly beautiful way of decorating a house, church or barn; they are also eminently practical arrangements on the kind of truly lavish scale that will totally transform a setting.

Country bunches and red rope make a simple but very effective display across the altar rail. Beneath the window a wide garland creates a tapestry of contrasting colours, while to the side of the altar a huge, free arrangement fills an awkward area of white space.

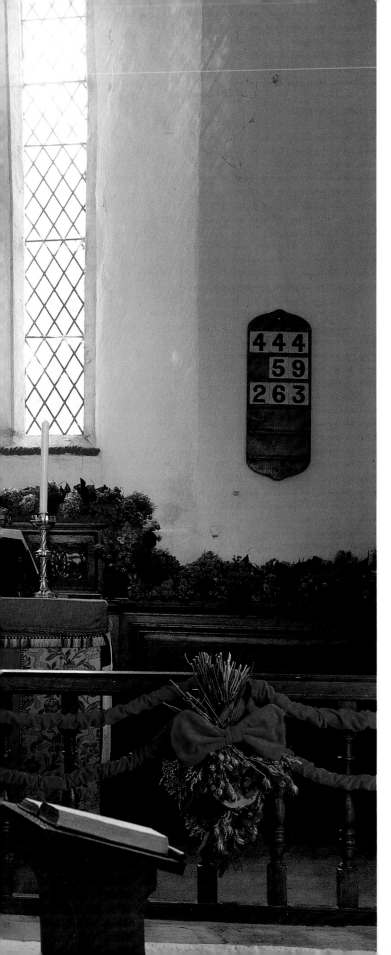

SPECIAL OCCASIONS

A winter wedding, a traditional Christmas celebration, a harvest or thanksgiving supper are just a few of the occasions when one is justified in going over the top with dried flowers. Used generously, they add a touch of magic and fantasy to any scene. And they're not just a spectacularly beautiful way of decorating a house, church or barn; they are also eminently practical arrangements on the kind of truly lavish scale that will totally transform a setting.

Country bunches and red rope make a simple but very effective display across the altar rail. Beneath the window a wide garland creates a tapestry of contrasting colours, while to the side of the altar a huge, free arrangement fills an awkward area of white space.

A WINTER WEDDING

A crisp winter's day, blue sky and sunshine. A twelfth-century church hidden down a quiet country lane. Brides-maids in red velvet dresses. And the interior of the church glowing with dried garlands and bunches of red roses massed with rich coppers, blues, green, pinks . . . These are the ingredients for a perfect winter wedding.

It's difficult to imagine a more charming location for a small wedding than the church of St James the Great at Idlicote, just a few miles down the road from Armscote. Built in the twelfth and late thirteenth centuries, it has a wealth of historical detail, including a large, high-sided pew where the local squire and his family would have sat out of sight of the lowlier members of the congregation. Another major feature, which we chose to highlight with our decorations, is the triple-decker pulpit. The sermon is read from the canopied top deck and the service taken from the lectern below. The lowest lectern, at the front of the pews, would originally have been occupied by the clerk who led the congregation. This area of the Cotswolds abounds with delightful churches, but few can rival the unspoilt charm of this one.

It's always saddened me that when it comes to special occasions, such as weddings, many people approach dried flowers as a last resort, a disappointing alternative to fresh flowers. I prefer to think of them as different, not second best. It's a bit like comparing the use of watercolours and oils in a painting. They're used in different ways for different effects. The same is true of dried flowers. Used creatively, dried flowers can offer tremendous scope for large-scale decorations. This is largely due to the fact that they're so practical to work with. All the arrangements you see in our pictures were made well in advance of the wedding day; we didn't have to worry about wilting and water-ing and all the other problems involved in working with fresh materials. And because we had the advantage of time, we could afford to be more lavish and imaginative than might otherwise have been the case.

Just a few words here about decorating churches. It's always advisable, no matter how low-key your flowers, to check with the clergyman concerned that it is all right for you to use them. There may be guidelines on the type of fixings you are allowed to use; some churches have been damaged by the indiscriminate hammering-in of nails and pins. If the church is a particularly busy one, there may also be a limit to the amount of time you have to put up and later remove the decorations between services. All these things should be taken into account before one starts plan-ning the flowers.

Once these details have been sorted out, one can move on to specific decisions, such as what colours to use. The fact that we were working with dried flowers in-fluenced our choice. We could have chosen to follow the traditional look and used pink roses, gypsophila, sea lavender, peonies, and larkspur to make pale, pretty arrangements. Instead we decided to go for something quite different; a spectrum of rich, glowing colours to provide warmth and brightness on a cold day. This is where dried flowers really come into their own. Their strong colours and textures can be used to create a kind of drama that is difficult to achieve with fresh materials. In these circumstances dried flowers aren't a substitute for the real thing – they're the first and best choice.

Looking for key themes on which to base the arrangements, we took into consideration the occasion and the style of the church and chose romantic red roses and bows, country bunches and warm-textured velvet. I find this technique of starting with a few basic elements very useful. Once the themes of a design have been established, the details then seem to fall quickly into place. I also find it useful to walk around the work-room and shop gathering a colour swatch of flowers and trying different combinations together until I have a small posy containing all the shades and forms that will be used. This is kept as a reference while we plan and make-up the arrangements. You can do this too, incorporating swatches of fabric and paint colours with small samples of dried flowers to work out a variety of combinations. A good dried flower shop should be happy to supply you with samples from which to choose.

Once we had decided upon our themes, colours and materials, we began designing the actual arrangements. For the altar rail, shown in the picture on pages 84-5, we used simple country bunches of single and spray red roses, nigella, sea lavender, dark red helichrysums, rust-coloured lupidium, green eucalyptus and large creamy-brown hoya leaves. These were trimmed with sumptuous wired bows of red velvet and hung along the altar rail at intervals. We added a long rope of ruched velvet to link them together, much of which was sewn by my husband, whose skill with the needle came as a great surprise! Each of the bunches was made by a member of the Armscote team, and although they all used the same materials they assembled them in slightly different ways. This was done deliberately. It's impossible to make two arrangements look exactly alike, so I prefer to use the differences positively and allow each its own character.

Something much larger was needed to fill the area of white space to the left of the altar and so we created an in-formal arrangement based around bunches of roses. We used both sprays of rambling roses and the larger individual blooms to give a variety of density and form. Glycerined green and copper beech branches were used

for height and volume, while the silver leaves of weeping pear can be seen at the bottom of the arrangement. Small bunches of oats and quaking grass gave a lift to the top, while the silver-white strands of seacrest helped break up the heavier foliage and provided a link with the white walls. The result is a big splash of rich, muted colour that boldly fills a difficult space.

I've found that it's best to build this kind of arrange-ment *in situ* so that one can judge exactly how large it needs to be for the best effect – which is usually much larger than originally anticipated. Remember that very few people are going to get close to it, so be brave and aim for a dramatic overall impression, like we did with the gazebo, rather than fine detail.

Across the carved screen and panelling behind the altar runs a wide garland packed with roses, both red and pink, hydrangeas in shades of purple, pale blue and light green, rust-coloured celosia, nigella, purple and mauve

A rich garland wound across the screen of the church helps to break-up the height of the arch and forms a glowing frame for the couple at the altar. The red velvet bows and the rope, used here and throughout the church, are touches of inspired colour that link all the arrangements together and contribute to the warm atmosphere in the church.

statice, pink African daisies, reddish-brown lupidium and lilac achillea, interspersed with glycerined poplar leaves dyed a strong blue-green. Here and there patches of sky-blue and pale pink reindeer moss fill up gaps between the flowers and add bright spots of unexpected colour that lift the darker hues of the garland. The result is a close-woven tapestry of colour and texture, full of contrasts and details.

A length of the same garland, interwoven with more of the red velvet rope, makes a spectacular feature of the carved wooden screen that spans the main arch. It can be appreciated in closer detail in the picture overleaf. Manoeuvring it into position and wrapping it at regular intervals across the screen was a major undertaking, but the garland stood up well to the stresses and strains. Remember another of the advantages of dried flowers is that they are more robust than they look. Whatever the effort, it was well worth it. The garland-covered screen provided a visual link between the two areas of the church and made a beautiful frame above the bride and groom at the altar.

The base of this broad garland is made of large-gauge chicken wire cut into a strip approximately 14 inches (35cm) wide. A word of warning is needed here as moulding chicken wire into shape can be a difficult process, so I would suggest wearing gardening gloves while you're handling it; especially as the cut ends can be very sharp. Tightly-packed dry sphagnum moss is then placed in the centre of the chicken wire and the edges folded inwards and secured, if necessary, with wire. This 'moss sausage' is flattened to make a firm, flat base about six inches (15cm) wide into which the flowers are wired. The final result is a reasonably flexible but secure garland, which will stand up to being twisted and pulled about without shedding its flowers.

Echoing this large garland is a narrower one that runs along the ledge in front of the choir stall. This was constructed on a mossed rope (see page 82 for details of how to make this kind of garland). It contains red roses, celosia, dark red helichrysums, blue-violet larkspur, nigella, pale pink African daisies and fronds of dried fern. Pale silver-blue poppy heads have been added for extra texture and interest. I like this idea of using two slightly different garlands in the same setting. Watching the people who came into the church while we were decorating it, I noticed how many of them examined the wide garland on the screen, compared it with the rope garland and then returned to the wide garland, to check its contents again. They would repeat this several times and each time they commented upon the differences their inspections had revealed.

When it comes to measuring up for garlands, I recommend using a rope, as I explained on page 82, since it's far easier to twine a rope around a screen or along a ledge and to measure off the length than it is to gauge it with a tape measure or ruler. I also find it helpful to take a few photographs at this stage, so that I can refer back to them if problems arise later. This is a particularly good idea if you can't keep returning to the place you're decorating. It's easy to forget the exact position of a pillar or a window. With a photograph for reference you can usually work out where you've gone wrong.

We used the rope technique for measuring up the swags that hang around the pulpit (see opposite) and

When there's a feature as splendid as this triple-decker pulpit, one simply has to make use of it. We did so with swags and narrow garlands that echo, but don't copy, the wide one overhead. For the panels of the old-fashioned box pews, alternating country bunches and bows add rustic simplicity and a touch of witty sophistication.

once the basic shape of each swag was established using roughly shaped pads made out of chicken wire, we wired in a selection of flowers. Clumps of dyed reindeer moss, secured with a wire bent into a simple U-shape were also added to the pad.

To break up the dull brown varnish of the box pews we hung alternating rows of bunches and bows along the panels. Like the swags, the basic shape of each bow was provided by a pad made out of chicken wire and moss and scrunched into shape. It's possible to achieve surprisingly detailed shapes using this technique. The bows were finished with long tails of red velvet.

Finally, the edge of the lower lectern was draped with another length of the rope garland, and further bunches were strategically placed to break up areas of white wall. When you're decorating a large and complicated space such as a church, it's always a good idea to take along more material than you think you will need – an extra length of garland, a few bunches, and a box of loose flowers may prove invaluable for filling an awkward gap. Despite advance planning there are always empty spaces and spots which need to be filled or concealed.

Our bridal bouquet, shown opposite, matches the strong statement made by the rest of our arrangements. It was packed with red roses, glycerined ivy, eucalyptus and beech leaves and large *Protea sulphurea*, with skeletal magnolia leaves. Bleached strelitzia and twisted cane gave it lightness and movement. It is boldly romantic and not for the faint-hearted. We designed it on a grand scale to sweep down to the feet of a tall bride, but a more restrained version would look just as good and one could use the same materials for making the bridesmaids' posies.

When making a bouquet like this, begin by establishing the length and general shape with foliage, gradually building up the layers and changing the angle of the flowers as you go. You may need to use several lengths of thick florists' wire joined together to achieve the right drop. Cover the wires with gutta percha (see page 134) to give them a neater finish. Gather all the wires and stalks at the back of the bouquet to make a handle and secure them into shape. Then cover the handle with gutta percha, line it with cotton wool or tissue paper and finally cover with ribbon. For fun and to echo the exposed stalks of the country bunches hanging on the pews, we added a false spray of stalks and a huge red bow to our bouquet. The end result was both dramatic and delightfully informal, a bouquet for making an unforgettable entrance to the church. And unlike one made from fresh flowers, it can be kept as a reminder of that perfect winter wedding.

To match the bouquet we made a simple, very free headdress from a wreath of lime twigs trimmed with celosia, stirlingia, fir cones, *Protea sulphurea*, pink and red miniature roses and touches of seacrest. This was decorated with another large velvet bow to be worn at the back or the side of the head. Dyed lichen moss was wired around the interior to allow a comfortable fit.

It's important when making a headdress like this to know how the bride intends to wear her hair on the wedding day and whether she will want to attach a veil. If this is the case, the veil can be sewn into the back of the circlet.

For a final touch to a perfect wedding, you might also like to consider decorating the church porch with a garland of flowers (see page 79).

This unashamedly romantic bouquet provides one of the finishing touches for the winter wedding. Though it takes its main colour inspiration from the red roses used elsewhere in the church, it is full of subtle contrasts.

Making the Arrangement

A BRIDE'S HEADDRESS

A coronet of flowers, whether fresh or dried, makes a classic and fashionable headdress for a bride and her bridesmaids. Be brave when making a circlet like this. Weddings are theatrical occasions and the headdress needs to be full and dramatic. It is the bride's crowning glory, not a last-minute afterthought. Experiment with different ways of wearing it until you find the angle that looks best, and remember to make the back just as beautiful as the front.

The circlet I'm demonstrating here incorporates the colours and materials we selected for the winter wedding, but you can use whatever you like when you make your own. When choosing materials, look for a variety of different textures and some contrasting colours. If you want to include the dense, velvety textures of moss and celosia, use something light and airy such as seacrest or gypsophila to balance them. If you choose pretty pinks as the basic colour, add sharp-green caustus or the silver-turquoise of baby eucalyptus.

Lime is particularly suitable for making the basic wreath, but you can use other types of pliable materials. A simple wire ring, completely covered with flowers and lichen, would be a perfectly good substitute.

MATERIALS REQUIRED
- *Lime twigs*
- *Stub and reel wire*
- *Scissors*
- *Gutta percha*
- *A velvet bow*
- *Roses, celosia, Decorum fir cones, Protea sulphurea, seacrest, fern and dyed reindeer moss*

1 Take a bunch of lime twigs and bend one to make a circle with a diameter of approximately 10-12 inches (25-30cm). Wire it into shape. Weave in further twigs, tucking them into position if possible, and wiring them only where necessary as it is important to keep the wiring to a minimum. Build up the circlet and trim any loose ends.

2 Add large-scale flowers, for example, seacrest, to the circlet. Divide materials such as celosia into florets. Wire-up small bunches of all the materials and cover the wires with gutta percha to conceal the joins. Combine individual small bunches to make sprays which are wired to the circlet at intervals.

3 Position the sprays at different angles so there is no obvious direction. Use materials at random so that the look is not too uniform. Add cones, Protea sulphurea and reindeer moss to cover the stalks and wires.

4 Stick or wire some more of the moss over any sharp interior twigs. Wire the bow into position at the back or side of the wreath.

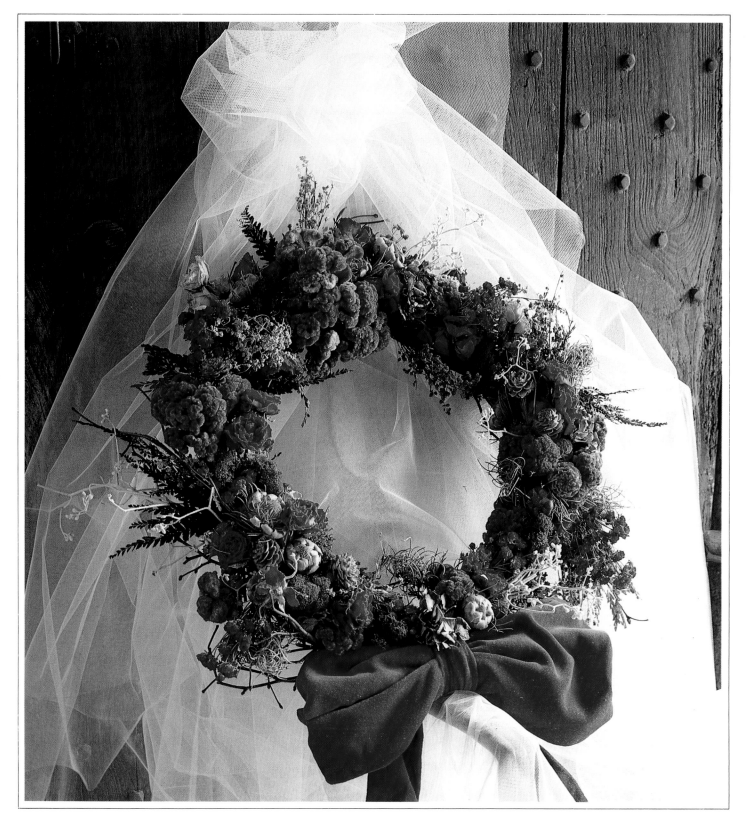

AN EASTER CELEBRATION

Yellow is the colour of springtime – of daffodils, prim-roses, chicks on Easter eggs, and warm sunshine after the long, dark, winter days – and so it's the obvious choice for Easter flowers. Very few of us go to such lengths to dec-orate our homes for the Easter festival as we do for Christ-mas, but it's still nice to mark the occasion. And the nicest way is with an arrangement or two for the breakfast or tea table on Easter Sunday.

Easter Sunday breakfast tends to be an informal affair, especially if you have children, and so I like the arrangements to reflect this relaxed atmosphere. It is also a great opportunity to make use of all those charming, mis-matched, amusing items of china that most of us have around our homes.

For our arrangements we collected together various pieces of country ware; a teapot, jugs and a biscuit barrel, all in the shape of cottages, an old jam pot, a pixie jug and a pitcher shaped like a cockerel. Interesting old mugs and cups and the kind of whimsical containers that are difficult to know what to do with the rest of the year all come in use-ful at Eastertime. So do eggcups. A very pretty display can be made using a variety of eggcups filled with dry foam and studded with flowers. Children love making this sort of simple arrangement. For something a little more special for an Easter guest, take a double eggcup and fill one side of it with flowers. In the other place a decorated boiled egg.

The photograph on the right demonstrates the easy and yet very attractive results one can achieve with the minimum of sophistication. On the left yellow helichry-sums, green glixia, lavender, phalaris, yellow-dyed gyp-sophila and creamy-white pearl achillea were combined to create this sunny effect. In front of it, another small jug was filled with yellow roses, purple larkspur, cluster-flowered *Helipterum sanfordii*, small-headed achillea, im-mortellum and oats. A third jug contains a mixture of this material combined with some strong green eucalyptus leaves to give the arrangement new colour and shape.

Small arrangements like these are an excellent way for a beginner to learn basic dried-flower arranging skills and develop confidence. For your first attempt at knitting you wouldn't start with a complicated Fairisle sweater, yet some people attempt the dried-flower equivalent. Fired with enthusiasm after seeing a splendid basket or bouquet, they set out to produce their own version. Disillusionment soon creeps in as they discover how long it takes to finish and how difficult it can be to balance colours, shapes and textures to obtain what originally seemed a very simple effect. It's far better to start on a less ambitious project such as these small arrangements, which enable you to ex-periment with colour and shape as you go along. And even more important than this, small arrangements that use a wide variety of materials allow you to become familiar with the way in which different flowers work in com-bination with one another. You can try out new and daring ideas safe in the knowledge that if they don't work you won't have wasted huge amounts of flowers and that it won't take long to put it right.

The photograph on pages 98-99 demonstrates a few more of the possible variations on the Easter theme. Beneath the cockerel, now boasting a magnificent tail of dried flowers, is a jam pot filled with a mushroom-shaped mound of glixia arranged in irregular-shaped patches – a simple concept but one which demands dexterity and good colour sense. The two cottage arrangements have had flax, botao, carthamus and alchemilla added to ring the

*Charming country-style jugs make ideal containers for bright, informal
Easter arrangements like these. Make a feature of them by grouping a
number together on a dresser or the breakfast table. Small-scale
arrangements are the best way of gaining flower-arranging experience,
allowing the beginner plenty of scope to experiment with colour and
shape whilst guaranteeing fast results.*

Variations on the Easter theme. Country cottages, plump yellow chicks and formal table arrangements are all linked by a common colour scheme and a few key materials.

changes. On the right is a more formal arrangement in a vase, showing how the same principles and materials can be used on a larger scale.

In the centre of the picture you'll see a large, low arrangement incorporating colourful polyanthus. This is our year-round table arrangement in its spring finery, ready to be used as a centrepiece on a dining-table or as an attractive, seasonal feature for elsewhere in the house.

The history of this arrangement, its constituents and the various ways in which it can be used are recounted in detail on page 114. Of course, you don't have to add polyanthus to it; any spring flowers or foliage will do. A combination of delicately scented narcissi, bright blue grape hyacinths and pink tulips would look wonderful. So would small sprigs of apple or cherry blossom and catkins. One advantage of using polyanthus is that, unlike cut flowers, they don't have to die to contribute their colour

and freshness to the arrangement. We took them from their pots, removed as much soil as possible from their roots and wrapped them gently in plastic film before adding them to the year-round arrangement. After several days they were taken out again and repotted, none the worse for their experience.

Finally we come to the most whimsical of all the Easter arrangements – our three plump yellow chicks in their nest. It's possible to make almost anything out of dried flowers, and what you make doesn't have to be serious or elegant. Teddy bears, rabbits, a model of the Empire State Building or a red London bus - there's no limit. Most arrangements of this kind are based on a frame made of chicken wire or a moss shape. In the case of our chicks, we started with two moss balls of different sizes, bound with reel wire. The two were combined to make the chick shape and then covered with individual florets of cluster-flowered helipterums which were stuck on with glue. A couple of small, pointed leaves were inserted to form the beak, and the eyes were made from the tiny seed heads of the field poppy, coloured black with a felt-tip pen.

Children are particularly enthusiastic about this literal use of dried flowers, which has a more immediate appeal for them than abstract arrangements. My daughter watched us taking hours over our nest of chicks and then produced a perfect specimen of her own in 15 minutes flat. And just to put us to further shame she also made it a little moss nest, in which it's sitting at this very moment in our kitchen waiting until it can assume pride of place next Easter!

A HARVEST FESTIVAL SUPPER

The barn shown on pages 106-107 is situated in the pretty village of Tredington just a mile or two down the road from Armscote. Usually it houses odd bits of furniture, bales of straw and the general bric-a-brac of farm life, but for special occasions it is cleared and used for parties. As soon as we saw its old beams and thatch we knew we'd found the perfect location for a harvest festival supper. Fortunately the barn's owners thought so too and very kindly allowed us to use it.

Dried flowers are a particularly appropriate medium for decorating a harvest festival. Like the fruit, vegetables and cereals on display, they're a tribute to nature's diversity and abundance. When it came to selecting flowers for the arrangements we bore this 'natural' theme in mind and deliberately tried to steer away from dyed, bleached or other 'unnatural' materials. We also tried to use the kind of autumn-tinted flowers one might expect to find in local cottage gardens and hedgerows, and aimed to make them into simple, unpretentious displays in keeping with the setting.

In order to achieve this we looked around for some simple, but rustic containers and, in keeping with the agricultural theme of the setting, agricultural tools. We were helped in our search for the latter by James Davis, an acquaintance who runs a marvellous antique shop in Shipston-on-Stour, our nearest town. He's a great enthusiast and collector of old agricultural implements and lent us some of his favourite items.

We started work in front of an old door, where the sunlight streaming through the gaps between the timbers created a wonderful pattern of light on our still-life grouping. Behind an old wheelbarrow filled with a variety of fresh vegetables we placed an apple tub packed with apples and decorated with bunches containing gnarled apple twigs, dark brown bracken, yellow broom and tufted phalaris. Next to it a basket taken from an old butcher's bicycle was filled with lavender. The front of the basket was trimmed with moss, bright yellow drumsticks of *Craspedia globosa* and dried delphiniums from the garden at Armscote.

Below it is one of the cheapest and simplest of all arrangements, a small wheatsheaf twisted, domed and tied with raffia. And proving my theory that one can use almost anything as a container and imaginative jumping-off point, the picture is completed by an old sack, something of a rarity in these days of plastic, topped with flowers – spray roses, poppy heads, oats, yellow daisies and *Limonium suworowii*, also known as pink poker. We stuffed the sack with newspapers to achieve the shape, then added a layer of crumpled chicken wire in which the flowers were inserted.

None of these arrangements required much expertise, time or money, yet all are effective. Perhaps the most distinctive harvest symbol of all is the wheatsheaf. Several sheaves, made in different sizes and of different cereals, grouped together would make a classic focus for a harvest thanksgiving service. Remember that the size of a sheaf is determined by its height. It's worth looking out for the taller varieties of wheat which will enable you to work on a larger scale.

There's another small wheatsheaf in the corner of the barn, but the attention here is focussed on two barrels decorated with wreaths of dried flowers, leaves and vegetables. It's the generous depth of these wreaths that make them look so good. Any narrower and they would have looked mean and insignificant. Any deeper and they would have been overwhelming.

Gauging proportions can be a difficult business, but I would always advise erring on the side of generosity. I think it's this that distinguishes the very best florists from the rest, both amateur and professional. The most dramatic and successful arrangements are those that very nearly go over the top. They are fuller, bigger, braver in colour and variety of materials than the rest. They make a strong, positive statement.

Bear this in mind when you are making an arrangement of your own. Nothing looks less interesting than a sparse scattering of flowers in boringly conventional complementary shades. Be brave and, when you think you've finished, try adding more flowers, some in a new and unexpected colour. Nine times out of ten the result is a great improvement on the original, and on the odd exception it's no great trouble to retrieve the basic arrangement and start all over again.

But back to our barrels. Both were prepared with a thick collar of dry sphagnum moss held in place by chicken wire which had been gathered and stapled, using a staple gun, to the inner rim. We then decorated one of the barrels in strong, autumn colours using golden helichry-

Dried flowers make an appropriate decoration for a harvest supper because, like so much of the fresh produce in the picture, many flowers and grasses are harvested for drying in the summer and early autumn. Of all the arrangements, the wheatsheaf is the quickest and easiest to make. Take a large bunch of wheat and tie it into a secure but slightly loose bundle. Now give the outer stems a firm twist so that they splay outwards in a spiral. Gradually push up the inner core of stems to create a softly rounded shape, then trim. Finish with raffia, a plaited straw garland or a paper bow.

sums, bright orange Chinese lanterns, yellow achillea and deep red celosia. The addition of brown bracken and oak leaves brought out the colour in the arrangement. Dark, sludgy, apparently unattractive colours often make the clearer, prettier colours around them sing. If you have a pretty but rather dull arrangement, try adding dark purple amaranthus, some deep copper beech leaves, rusty-purple dock or dark-dyed broom bloom and see what happens.

For the second barrel we used a quite different approach. Decorated in cool blues and greys with a sharp yellow, the result was sophisticated and muted: a contrast to the bright, sunny colours of the other arrangement. Dried artichokes, poppy heads and garlic all added to its strong sculptural qualities. The lemon helichrysums and verticordia formed a link with the other barrel, but the addition of lilac achillea, pale oats and dyed blue broom bloom changed the mood completely.

When planning a number of arrangements that will be grouped together, as here, it's tempting to stick to the same colours throughout so that everything is co-ordinated. The result can be pleasant but dull. Always include an occasional contrast, like this garlic-laden garland, to throw everything into perspective.

You don't have to be a colour expert to devise interesting combinations, but a little knowledge of the colour spectrum and the way it works can be useful. Generally speaking, colours that lie next to each other in the spectrum give a pleasing, low-key effect when used together. Thus, orange and yellow, yellow and green, green and blue, blue and violet, violet and red, and red and orange will blend harmoniously with each other. Colours a little further apart in the spectrum also combine well, but with a stronger contrast. Yellow and blue, green and violet, red and yellow, and orange and green, for example, are all striking and subtle combinations.

Most striking of all, and generally recommended only for the brave, are those colours which are furthest apart in the spectrum. Yellow and violet, red and green, and orange and blue combinations, will all result in startlingly dramatic effects that are best used with caution. These strong combinations are known as complementary colours; red is the complementary colour of green, and so on. To find out why they should be so called, try adding a red rose to a bunch of green eucalyptus leaves. The rose will make the eucalyptus appear even more green and will itself appear to be a truer red. The same is true of the yellow-violet and orange-blue combinations.

Complementary colours are particularly useful when you are trying to create special effects. A basket filled with orange dahlias, helichrysums and chinese lanterns, for example, will look brighter and more fiery if it is placed against a blue background, or if a few blue delphiniums are arranged among the other flowers.

This kind of attention to colour and contrast is all to be commended, but remember, as I mentioned before, when it comes to designing for a large space, like the barn, one must try not to get carried away with details at the expense of the overall scene. If it helps try and think of it as designing a stage set and use broad strokes to fill out the background, reserving the finer touches for the fore-

Though the dominant shades of harvest are warm yellow, gold and orange, the occasional introduction of a contrasting colour, as here in the cool white of the garlic and blue of the poppy heads and verticordia on the upper barrel, helps to sharpen and dramatize the main theme. The imaginative flower arranger is constantly experimenting with colour, adding muted shades to pretty pastels and looking for strong or subtle contrasts.

*A perfect setting for a harvest
supper, the table framed by the
informal sweep of a hay garland*

ground. Looking at the area in which we intended to site the supper table we realized that a large arrangement would be needed to fill the wall behind, and that something was required to link the beam over the table to everything going on beneath it.

Our solution for the wall was an arrangement of farm implements, wired together to make a rustic sculpture. This was based on a wooden backboard padded with moss and covered in chicken wire. We slung it on ropes over the beams, thus avoiding the use of screws or nails which might have damaged the fabric of the barn. Working *in situ* so that he could judge the best proportions and angles, it took Simon Lycett, one of a breed of new, young and necessarily athletic florists, only half an hour to attach the sieves, pitchforks, rakes and other implements using heavy gauge florists' wire. The outlines were softened with bunches of wheat while others, containing achillea, helichrysums, Chinese lanterns and phalaris, added colour.

For the beam above the table we made a hay garland. Of all the various forms of garland this is the quickest and easiest to make, requiring nothing more than a quantity of hay and plenty of thin silver reel wire. If you'd like to make one yourself, start by taking a good handful of hay, teasing it out into a bulky rope and winding it with a spiral of reel wire. Position the loops of wire close enough together to hold the garland firmly, yet not so close that they become visible or make the garland too tight and rigid. Keep adding more handfuls of hay as you go along, easing out the rope shape and binding with wire. When you have the right length, tie the wire off tightly, then wind more of it back along the garland in the opposite direction.

This last step is important, as you'll discover if you should forget it. A hay garland is meant to be reasonably free and informal, but without a second strand of wire it will probably fall apart when you try to hang it up. No matter how well-made the garland, you may also find that it stretches, particularly if you attach anything to it. We fixed ours quite tightly, allowing for a few inches of droop when we added bunches of flowers to it. Our finished garland spiralled down the post supporting the beam, forming a frame for the table below.

The table itself is decorated with more bunches of helichrysums, sea lavender, bright yellow African daisies and golden broom bloom, tucked among the loaves that are displayed, appropriately enough, in old dough troughs. In the centre of the table is a low, mounded basket arrangement holding a combination of dried and seasonal fresh flowers. This is another version of the 'year-round' table arrangement which was invented, as its name suggests, to provide changing colour throughout the year. Basically it is a basket arrangement of sea lavender, alchemilla, nigella and white larkspur, flowers chosen for their variety of form and low-key colours that will complement a wide range of additions. To this basic arrangement may be added seasonal dried and fresh flowers to create an impressive display that's particularly useful as a centrepiece for a dining-table.

Filling an awkward stretch of wall can be difficult. Here the problem is
solved with a collection of old agricultural tools hung together and
trimmed with dried flowers and wheat. These small touches demonstrate
how easy it is to bring colour and light to what could have been a lifeless
display. You can use the same technique to brighten your own home. Try
hanging a colourful tied bouquet from the end of a plain bedstead or a
cupboard doorhandle, or brighten a static collection of baskets, pottery
or copperware by adding simple bunches of home-dried garden flowers.

*The harvest table, decorated with simple country bunches of wheat,
oats, gold and bronze helichrysums, sea lavender and yellow daisies. In
the centre of the table is the year-round arrangement, a combination of
dried and fresh flowers that can be varied throughout the year.*

There are two obvious advantages to this type of multi-purpose arrangement. First, it is quick and easy to use and doesn't require any great skill. One simply has to snip off the fresh flowers and insert them directly into the plastic foam base, where they will last for a day or two. Or, if you prefer, small plastic or glass florists' vials can be buried in the foam and filled with water. Fresh flowers placed in these will last much longer. Whichever technique you choose, it takes just a few minutes to create a densely-packed basket that looks as if hours have been spent on it.

Secondly, it's economical. In an ideal world no one would approach the subject of flowers with a budget in mind. The best arrangements, fresh or dried, are generous in scale and content and very often in expense, too. My business experience, however, has taught me that for most people cost is a significant factor. The joy of this arrangement is that a few fresh flowers go a long way and look surprisingly impressive. Using the dried material as a base, it's possible to have a large and eye-catching arrangement that changes its appearance from week to week and season to season, yet doesn't break the bank.

For the harvest festival table we added fresh trumpet-shaped orange alstroemeria and apricot spray chrysanthemums, and dried bracken and poppy heads, all of which gave a warm, autumnal feel. The alstroemeria and chrysanths were temporary additions, but there are other fresh flowers that once inserted into vials or foam will slowly dry out and become a permanent part of the arrangement. Hydrangeas, heather, statice, helichrysums and African proteas, among others, will all dry attractively if left in place. One word of warning. If you choose to use vials to hold the fresh flowers, fill them carefully and try not to get the dried flowers wet, otherwise they will rot.

Most of the arrangements and ideas we devised for the harvest festival can be adapted to suit other occasions, too. Though Thanksgiving is usually a more formal affair than a harvest supper, many of the arrangements you see on these pages can be easily adapted for a smarter interior setting. Take some of the simple bunches, for example, that decorate our table, and arrange them in a container – or hang one on a ribbon from the back of each chair around a dining-table. Take the hay garland (page 108), cover it with Chinese lanterns, small bunches of wheat and corn on the cob and drape it around a door or across the table. Instead of garlanding barrels or baskets, use flowers to decorate ceramic platters or bowls – the garlands can be held in place with tape and removed without damaging the container. A row of wheatsheaves in diminishing sizes ranged across a sideboard will look great. Or for something a little different, take the idea of the lavender arrangement on page 101 and adapt it, filling a simple Shaker-influenced wooden box with upright sprigs. Lavender is, in fact, an appropriate flower for Thanksgiving. It was the brightest colour that the Quakers were traditionally allowed to wear. In this way, developing your own associations and bringing your own ideas to bear, you can adapt almost all the arrangements to suit a specific occasion or a more formal style.

The barn would also make a wonderful setting for a summer party or barn dance, for example, and to ring the changes one doesn't have to do much more than change the colour scheme. For a midsummer night's celebration, shown on page 113, we chose zinging pink, red, yellow and blue that gave quite a different feel to the supper table.

The bunches arranged in the dough troughs were replaced with new ones containing oats, sea lavender, pink helichrysums and dark blue larkspur. A plain apple basket became a work of art, its handle bound with a moss garland covered in vivid red roses, yellow mimosa, delphiniums, alchemilla, touches of yellow achillea and bright orange gomphrenas. More gomphrenas were combined with yellow roses and blue delphiniums for bow-tied bunches at the sides.

A large platter-shaped basket full of strawberries was encircled with a garland that illustrates two separate moods. At the back, orange Chinese lanterns positively sizzle among delphiniums and red roses, very neatly illustrating my earlier point about how well complementary colours can set each other off. The other half of the garland is rather more subdued in colour, but attractive nevertheless. Yellow roses and achillea, pale delphiniums and nigella are offset by pink titree.

In the right-hand corner of the picture, completely transformed by the addition of fresh roses, sweet peas and foliage from the garden at Armscote, is the year-round table arrangement in a summery incarnation. It looks wonderful, and I am particularly pleased with the way in which the basic ingredients have accommodated such a major shift in colour. What better centrepiece could one ask for the perfect midsummer night's supper table?

Midsummer magic. Raspberries and strawberries were the inspiration for this midsummer night's variation on the harvest theme. Replace the warm golden tones of autumn with the sizzling colours on the summer garden and you have baskets and garlands so vibrant they almost dazzle the eye. In the corner, transformed with roses and sweet peas picked fresh from the gardens at Armscote, is the year-round table decoration in its midsummer finery.

Making the Arrangement

A YEAR-ROUND DECORATION

The year-round arrangement is designed for people who like their flowers to change from week to week and season to season. It is a basic basket loosely filled with low-key flowers that make a good background for the fresh and seasonal dried flowers that are added throughout the year. In designing it we originally intended it to make a useful centrepiece for a dining-table, but it could be used anywhere you need an unusual feature.

Fresh flowers can be added to the dry foam base, where they will last for a day or two, depending on variety. To make them last longer, you can insert a number of florists' vials into the foam and fill them with water using an eye dropper, or wrap the stems in damp moss and place the fresh flowers into them.

This arrangement has its advantages. It is constantly changing and so one never becomes bored with it (though of course you can always adapt dried-flower arrangements if you become tired of them). And with just a few fresh flowers you can very quickly achieve an impressive, colourful arrangement that would have required time and a large quantity of fresh material to produce from scratch.

MATERIALS REQUIRED
- *Medium-sized oval basket*
- *Dry foam blocks*
- *Scissors and a knife*
- *Stub wires*
- *Florists' vials (optional)*
- *Sea lavender, nigella, alchemilla, white larkspur*

1 Cut the dry foam blocks to size and secure them inside the basket using stub wires bent into a U-shape. If you wish to use plastic vials for holding the fresh flowers, it is best to insert them at random in the foam at this stage.

2 Take all the dried materials and cut and wire them into individual bunches by trimming the stems to within a few inches of the flower heads. (Further instructions for wiring bunches can be found on page 118.) Start inserting one variety at random.

3 Build up the arrangement using the other materials. In this case the basic flowers are nigella, sea lavender, alchemilla and white larkspur.

4 The finished arrangement is quite loose, to allow for the addition of fresh and seasonal material when required. It can be adapted to create an arrangement for Easter, Christmas, Autumn or Summer.

For Easter we chose to add brightly-coloured polyanthus to the basic arrangements, but there are innumerable alternatives for the early months of the year. Try hyacinths or narcissi for fragrance, scarlet tulips and golden daffodils for cheerful colour, amaryllis for drama or delicate apple and cherry blossom for a subtle, truly seasonal, appeal.

Oranges, holly and sprigs of yew were our Christmas additions, but they're not the only options. Spruce, pine cones and Christmas roses would give a more traditional effect: vibrant red poinsettias or rust-red chrysanthemums offer intense colour; and for fun one could insert Christmas tree baubles, tiny presents and touches of glitter.

For additional autumn colour we added orange alstroemeria and apricot-coloured chrysanthemums to the dried material. Other seasonal alternatives include dahlias, sedums, winter-flowering jasmine, passion flowers, blackberry brambles, sprigs of berry-covered pyracantha and autumn-tinted foliage.

The midsummer garden is so full of superb flowers that we were spoiled for choice! In the end we chose dazzling sweet peas and red spray roses, which both look and smell wonderful, to add to the basic arrangement. Scented stocks, cornflowers, sweet William, honeysuckle, jasmine, poppies, fresh alchemilla, lavender, gypsophila would all make truly delightful summer additions.

A COTSWOLD MANOR CHRISTMAS

Every old house has its own individual character, and for our Christmas setting we wanted to find somewhere we could decorate on a grand scale. A tall ceiling to accommodate a big Christmas tree and a large fireplace for an open log fire were the first two requirements on our list. We found these and many more delights at a manor house just a few miles from Armscote. Approached through apple orchards and an avenue of walnut trees, it has an imposing but friendly atmosphere. Its vast wood-panelled hall overlooked by an impressive gallery combines formality with a lived-in feel. This is the perfect home for a traditional Christmas.

Finding our location was one thing. Finding fresh ideas for the arrangements was something else entirely. Other books seem to skip over this difficult, head-scratching stage of the creative process and pretend that original ideas flow freely. I'd like to put the record straight. Occasionally one does have a blinding flash of insight, but most of the time it's just plain hard work that eventually results in a good idea. As usual when stuck for ideas we had a brainstorming session and asked ourselves what kind of themes we associated with Christmas.

Holly, ivy, mistletoe, Santa Claus, reindeer and pine cones immediately sprung to mind – nothing very original there. A partridge in a pear tree was a possibility, but how could we use the theme to decorate the whole hall? Christmas stockings seemed too naive for such a sophisticated setting, but the idea stuck with us. We thought a little harder. What does one find in a Christmas stocking? Oranges. This led to thoughts of mulled wine and the heady scent of oranges and cloves. And one just had to put oranges and cloves together to have the spicy, Christmassy fragrance of pomanders. At last we had our Christmas

theme and one that was sharper and more sophisticated than the usual red, green and silver colour scheme, yet just as traditional in its own way and ideally suited to the character of our setting.

Oranges were also a good choice for another reason. When using flowers on a grand scale like this, it can help to include some large, bold materials that will add strong colour and drama to simple and relatively plain arrangements. In this way you can reduce the amount of detailed work required, a great saving on time and effort. By using oranges, tartan bows and bunches of small red glass baubles for our 'strokes' of bright colour, and a background of subdued dark greens and reds for the basic arrangements, we hoped to achieve a good contrast of depth and brightness.

It's a long haul from having the original ideas to realizing them, of course, and if you are embarking on a major series of arrangements I would strongly recommend you begin work on one of the smaller items. It's both physically and emotionally easier to solve any problems you encounter if you're working on a small scale. I know from experience how disheartening it is to have to 'unmake' a large arrangement. Once you've ironed out any unexpected hitches – colours not working as planned, awkward textures or unexpected effects – you can move on to the larger items.

Our troubleshooting arrangement was the wreath, shown on page 119. This was constructed on a commercial wire wreath frame that we covered with moss, bound in place with reel wire. The background material was spiky sea lavender, wired into place and then sprayed a dark, slightly glossy green using a paint gun. I use this method for many of the Christmas arrangements we make at

Armscote, and for several reasons. Sea lavender is cheap and easy to work with and, once sprayed, gives an excellent effect. The dark green paint is a more traditional and useful colour than some of the shades of dried foliage available. If you'd like to try out this idea yourself, you can do so by using aerosol paint to spray the sea lavender. Over this base we wired dark green kunzea, overlaid with bright green and deep red-brown amaranthus. To this were added knots of poppy seed heads and fir cones which can either be stuck in position or wired in place using heavy gauge stub wire.

If you decide to use wire for the fir cones, simply push one end of the wire through the lowest scales, circle it tightly around the cone and then twist the two ends together. Use scissors or wire cutters to trim the shorter end, if necessary, and use the longer one to attach the cone to the wreath.

To make the clusters of poppy seed heads or any other kind of flowers, take a small bunch of the material and cut the stems to within three inches (7.5cm) of the flower heads. Hold a stub wire vertically against the stems, aligning the end of the wire with them. With the other hand, take the wire round behind the stems about one inch (2.5cm) below the flower heads. Now twist the long end of the wire down round the stems in a spiral, covering the shorter end as you go. Use the long end of the wire as a stalk to stick into dry foam, or to bind the bunch tightly to a wreath or garland. Wiring a bunch is one of the fundamental techniques of dried-flower arranging, yet it's surprisingly difficult to master at first. Everyone seems to develop their own, highly individual, methods to make it easier, but it takes plenty of practice to discover them. It's worthwhile, however, as it enables you to achieve a thick, tight cluster of flowers on a single flexible stem which is far easier to work with than individual, brittle-stemmed flowers. Wired bunches can make all the difference to low,

dense arrangements which will look smooth and tightly-packed, with nothing visible but flower heads. Without them one tends to get a loosely filled arrangement through which stalks and too often patches of dry foam can be seen.

Returning to the next stage of our Christmas wreath, we added cinnamon sticks, wired in small bundles, and tartan bows to the fir cones, glass balls and poppy heads. The arrangement was made-up in advance and we added the satsumas at the last minute by simply piercing them with a long stub wire, twisting the ends together and using the long end to secure the fruit to the wreath. The smell was quite intoxicating and soon had everyone humming Christmas carols. Wired like this, fruit will last for at least a week before rotting, much longer if conditions are warm and dry enough for it to dry out. After Christmas the oranges, so long as they are not rotten, are quite safe to consume if the part through which the wire has passed is cut out.

Around the doorframe we hung a simple rope garland covered in kunzea, fern and sprigs of blue spruce and yew. The latter will dry extremely well if given a good spray of a fixative such as hair lacquer or one of the commercial products sold to prevent Christmas trees dropping their needles. The blue spruce of the garland ties in with the large, mounded arrangement on the circular table. This dense tapestry of colour and texture was made using kunzea and amaranthus, studded with bunches of blue-green and glowing red verticordia, dark brown oak leaves, fresh variegated holly, yew and masses of trailing ivy. Among this oranges, glass balls and fir cones contribute to the free, richly-coloured effect.

The fragrances of the oranges and the pine needles combine in these arrangements to create an instantly festive mood

Its qualities are best appreciated from a short distance, as the picture on the previous two pages shows. Here one can appreciate the effect of all the arrangements together. I must say that it really was a spellbinding scene; the kind of Christmas setting one dreams of but doesn't expect to see. It is difficult to know quite where to begin describing it, but I should perhaps start at the fireplace which we draped with another length of rope garland wired with oranges and satsumas. I draw your attention to this because I am always nervous of using dried flowers near candles and fires. One can minimize the risks by applying a flame-proofing spray to the arrangements, but I have seen for myself how quickly dried flowers can catch light and I would still urge caution.

Caution was not in evidence, however, when we decorated the magnificent Christmas tree. Here I must thank my great friend Hamish Greycheap, who supplied it at such short notice. We covered this splendid specimen with decorations, many of them containing dried flowers. Particularly attractive are the small red and green cane wreaths, each with a spray of flowers. Should you feel that we have cheated by using a fresh Christmas tree for our pictures, turn to page 126 and you'll find illustrated instructions on how to make one from dried foliage and flowers. Unfortunately six feet is about the height limit; after that one requires such large branches of dried material that their weight becomes too much to deal with. If you have a room as large as the one seen here, I'm afraid there is no option but to choose a fresh Christmas tree.

Dried flowers provide the backdrop for a classic Christmas Eve scene. There are presents around the tree, chestnuts in a basket by the fire, candles flickering on the mantelpiece and, no doubt, carol singers outside the front door.

On the table in front of the tree is the familiar shape of the year-round centrepiece arrangement (described in detail on page 114). For its Christmas appearance it strikes a suitably festive note, studded with oranges and covered with sprigs of holly and yew. Yew berries are both poisonous and extremely attractive to children, so take great care when including them in an arrangement and be prepared to omit them if necessary.

Another arrangement full of seasonal materials is the garden trug at the foot of the chair. It contains walnuts gathered from the trees that line the approach to this house and is decorated very simply with fir cones and long cinnamon sticks. The cones have been scented with a few drops of spicy essential oil so that they release a rich fragrance which combines well with the sharpness of the oranges.

The fruit-filled basket placed on the table with its delightfully fragrant pomanders, adds to the heady atmosphere of the room. Though they're wonderful to have around the house at any time of year, pomanders have always been associated with Christmas and make wonderful decorations. To make pomanders yourself you will need firm, unblemished oranges or apples, a good store of high-quality, large-headed cloves and a thick darning needle for piercing holes.

Make holes at regular intervals all over the fruit, inserting the cloves as you go. Leave a gap of about a quarter of an inch (0.6cm) between the cloves so that the skin doesn't split. If you intend to hang the pomander on a ribbon, leave a clove-free channel, half an inch wide (1.2cm), around its middle. This will hold the ribbon neatly in place. To prevent the pomanders from rotting they must be 'cured' in a spice mixture for a period of two weeks or more. The following recipe will give enough of the mixture to cure several pomanders at once. It can be re-used many times. In a large bowl mix together the following ingredients: 2oz (50g) of powdered cloves, 4oz (100g) of powdered cinnamon, 1 dessertspoon of powdered nutmeg, 1 dessertspoon of powdered allspice and 1oz (25g) of powdered orrisroot. Place the pomanders in this mixture and turn them gently so that they are completely covered. Continue to turn them each day, ensuring they are well dusted with spices, until they are hard and shrunken. Remove them from the mixture, dust them off and use them as you like. Piled in a bowl in the living-room or hanging in a wardrobe, they will perfume the air with a rich, spicy but fresh scent that everyone will appreciate. Pomander-making is the kind of task that children enjoy, and the fruits of their labours, if they can bear to part with them, make very acceptable presents. Next time they complain that they have nothing to do, why not sit them down with oranges, cloves and small knitting needles and introduce them to this ancient art?

When we were planning our arrangements for the gallery we considered making bunches of ribboned pomanders and hanging them from the broad posts spaced along it at intervals. Eventually this idea was dropped in

The gallery. Seen from straight on, the orange trees and central swag of the garland frame the tapestry, creating a pleasing symmetry. Arrangements like these take time to make, but when you have a feature worth highlighting, such as this, they're worth it. Once made, they can be used for several years, and by varying their contents they can be brought out for occasions other than Christmas. Remove the oranges, cones, ribbons and glass baubles and replace them with roses, lavender, white larkspur and blue delphiniums, for example, and you have beautiful arrangements for a wedding or a party.

favour of the solution you can see on the previous page. Three broad garlands containing our key materials — oranges, fir cones, ribbons, poppy heads and shining red baubles — were suspended across the balustrade. Because the central span was wider than those on either side we deliberately gave the middle garland a deeper drop. The width of its span just happened to be the same as the width of the beautiful old tapestry that hangs on the gallery wall. As if the combination of these two elements wasn't enough, we topped each of the gallery's main posts with an orange tree to create a frame for the tapestry. The symmetry of this design suited the formality of the hall, once again illustrating the importance of using flowers that complement the character of the setting.

We measured the required length of garland, as on previous occasions using a rope, and like the broad garland in the church, it was made using moss-filled chicken wire. Before we began adding the flowers and foliage we marked its centre. Then we began working at each end and moved inwards towards the centre. This is a point worth remembering if your material has a definite direction and you want a symmetrical look to the finished arrangement. Our materials for the garlands and the orange trees were the same as those for the wreath, green-sprayed sea lavender with kunzea and two different colours of amaranthus.

All the arrangements on these pages can be stored and re-used year after year, so none of the trouble (and pleasure) of making them is wasted. Perishable material such as the oranges should be removed before the arrangements are put away in boxes at the end of the season. Store them in a dry place and, if you can obtain them, add a sachet or two of silica gel to the boxes before they are closed (see page 132). These will absorb any excess moisture in the air and ensure that the dried material stays dry. Each year you can ring the changes by adding new and different touches to the basic garlands. For example, small Christmas crackers and gift-wrapped parcels could be wired in for a brighter effect; Chinese lanterns and gold-sprayed cones would give a cheerful yet subtle display; or you could look around your home and locality for your own sources of inspiration.

If you find the prospect of making garlands and Christmas trees a daunting one, then you may be reassured to know that there are other, simpler, arrangements at the opposite end of the scale. As the picture on the right shows, even the smallest of dried-flower bunches has its uses at Christmas. We used tiny off cuts of white gypsophila, each trimmed with a green leaf, some red glixia and a ribbon, to decorate the branches of the Christmas tree. Other tree arrangements include tiny cane wreaths, available from all good dried-flower supply shops (see page 135), spray-painted red and green and decorated with a few strands of sea lavender, a helichrysum and a small cone. These can be used to decorate not just the tree but the gifts around it. Other trimmings for special Christmas presents include large fir cones decorated with spirals of ribbon, strands of moss and an assortment of berries and flowers. Small decorations like this are an ideal way of using up the odd flowers and leaves left when you have finished a larger arrangement and provide the finishing touch to any gift.

The finishing touch to Christmas presents. Tiny bunches of dried flowers, made from off cuts from previous arrangements, are tied with ribbon or added to small cane rings to make gift trimmings. Pine cones too large to be hung from the tree or used in arrangements are decorated with moss, ribbon, berries and flowers to make spectacular gift tags.

Making the Arrangement

A CHRISTMAS TREE

A dried-flower Christmas tree makes a practical and attractive alternative to the real thing. It's far nicer to have around than a plastic tree, it doesn't shed its needles, and it can be put away on Twelfth Night and saved for the following year.

At Armscote we make thousands of Christmas trees of all shapes and sizes each year. One of our methods for the smaller trees is to use spiky sea lavender as the basic foliage. Once the tree has been covered with it, the whole thing is spray-painted a dark, faintly glossy green. We use a paint gun but aerosol paint is just as good. The result is excellent.

For larger trees one needs larger materials and the idea of spraying becomes less practical. The basic foliage of the tree shown here is dark green kunzea, but there are various alternatives available. Yew and spruce also dry well and would make very appropriate foliage.

I would advise strongly against using lights on this type of tree. Even though dried material can be sprayed with a flame retardant to make it fireproof, I think it is an unnecessary risk. And bear in mind that because the tree isn't very strong, any decorations you hang from it should be fairly lightweight.

The finished Christmas tree, complete with garland

MATERIALS REQUIRED

- *Large terracotta pot*
- *Sharpened branch*
- *16 four-inch nails and hammer*
- *Thistle plaster*
- *Expanded polystyrene packaging bubbles*
- *Dry foam blocks and cone*
- *Scissors and a knife*
- *Tape*
- *Stub and reel wires*
- *Ribbon and trimmings*
- *Kunzea, orsparsa, white titree, bupleurum, sphagnum moss, forest moss, reindeer moss, fir cones, gypsophila, glixia, Nigella orientalis*

1 Sharpen one end of a large branch, hammer in 16 large nails, as shown in the picture, and set the branch in thistle plaster (see page 69). Impale blocks of dry foam on the nails.

2 Attach a foam cone on the top of the branch. Use glue and tape, if necessary, to hold all the foam firm. Outline the shape of the tree by adding the basic foliage.

3 Continue to add the green foliage and highlight here and there with clusters of white. I used bupleurum and white titree, both of which have solid, woody stems that can be easily inserted into the foam. Finish the pot with a layer of sphagnum moss.

4 When the tree is ready, make a garland for it. A dried tree becomes less of a fake and more of a concept if decorated with dried materials. Use grey forest moss and bind it into a garland with reel wire. Wind tartan ribbon round it. We also added a long string of shiny red beads, available from the haberdashery departments of most stores.

5 Wire together tiny bunches of flowers – I used bleached gypsophila and red glixia, finished with a seed head of Nigella orientalis. *Conceal the wire with a ribbon and add each bunch to the garland.*

6 Add the finishing touches – pieces of dyed, light green reindeer moss, secured with a short U-shaped wire and white-sprayed fir cones.

A RESOURCE GUIDE

If the previous chapters of this book have inspired you to dry your own flowers, or make your own arrangements, you'll find this section useful. It contains practical information on methods of drying a wide range of material at home, on suppliers of dried flowers, on the tools of the trade and on plant names, which often cause confusion. Like all arts, arranging dried flowers has to be practised to be learned. I hope this information will make the learning process easier — and I hope that, like me, you will discover in dried flowers a source of great pleasure and self-expression.

Some of the wide selection of materials and accessories available at the Armscote Manor shop. Though there is an extensive range of flower-arranging equipment on the market, beginners need only a basic kit of florists' scissors, a long-bladed knife, stub wires and dry foam to get started.

DRYING YOUR OWN FLOWERS

There are various methods of drying flowers, some more suited to certain types of material than others. But before describing the processes, a few words on picking your own flowers for drying. Most flowers, particularly roses and peonies, are best picked just before they come into full bloom. Don't wait until they are fully open. If you do, they will shed their petals as they dry. Pick only the best flowers and ignore any that are diseased or badly blemished. It is best to harvest them in fine weather, not when they are still damp from rain or dew, and hang them as soon as possible.

Air Drying

Air drying is the simplest and most common means of preserving flowers and other types of plant material. When we grew and dried large quantities of material at Armscote in the early days of the business, it was the main method of preservation we used. I still air dry flowers cut from the garden, either in our kitchen or in the loft space above the work-room.

The main requirement for this process is a warm, dry area with plenty of circulating air. If it's dark, too, it will help preserve the colour of the flowers. Don't hang flowers where they will be in direct sunlight. During the summer a loft makes an ideal hanging place. Failing this a dry garage or shed, a spare room, a boiler room or an airing cupboard will do. The temperature should be a minimum 10°C, 50°F.

When you have found a suitable place and cut your flowers, remove the lower leaves and tie the material into manageable bunches – four or five stems is enough for most plants. I find rubber bands useful for holding bunches together. They grip the stems as they dry out and shrink. If you are using twine, bind the bunches tightly or stems may fall to the floor when dry. Large flowers and seed heads (artichokes and onion heads, for example) and plants with dense foliage should be strung individually. Most material can then be simply hung upside down from nails or a line, or on a rack – an old clothes horse is ideal – to dry. Don't hang the bunches too closely together or overload the space. Air must be able to circulate around and between the material so that moisture can evaporate. Large-headed material, including artichokes and maize, can be laid out to dry on sheets of newspaper or on a layer of chicken wire stretched over a fruit box. Stick the stems through the chicken wire so that the heads dry in an upright position.

In my experience almost all flowers and plants can be air dried, even delicate material such as daffodils. Experiment with the contents of your garden and see what happens. The very worst is that the petals will drop off – not much of a loss if one remembers that the flower would have died anyway.

Moss and lichen should also be dried by this method. Place them in a loose single layer in a wooden fruit box or lay them out on sheets of crumpled newspaper. Don't pack them tightly or they will rot.

You can tell your flowers are dry when they become papery and their stems have shrunk. The process can take from between a week to a month or longer, depending on the materials and the conditions in which they are kept. The bigger, fleshier and more dense the material – artichokes and onion heads, for example – the slower the process. Don't be tempted to save time by taking flowers down before they are completely dry. Petals will fall out and the whole stem may begin to rot.

Some flowers will do better if the air drying process is started while they are in water – a contradictory but successful method. Hydrangeas, gypsophila, proteas, statice, mimosa and achillea all dry well if they are put upright in half an inch of water and then placed in the drying area. By the time the water has been absorbed, the flowers are likely to be dry.

Glycerine

I use glycerine for preserving foliage. I like to have a good supply of preserved ivy, beech and oak leaves throughout the year and this is the best way of keeping them. Like air drying, the basic technique is quite simple if you have the space and time to do it properly.

Mix two measures of hot water with one measure of glycerine and add a few inches of this concoction to a tall container. Take freshly cut branches or strands of ivy and place the cut ends in it. They will absorb it and become preserved in the process. Top up the container as required. As the glycerine is absorbed and rises through the twigs and leaves, you may be able to observe their gradual change in colour. When all the leaves have undergone this change you can remove the branch and use it in your arrangements. The length of time this process takes depends very much on the type of material you are drying. To speed it up and generally improve absorption, crush woody stems or cut them at an acute angle before inserting them into the glycerine mixture.

As for suitable materials, I make a practice of regularly experimenting with new types of foliage. Catkins, old man's beard, ferns, eucalyptus, pin oak, smoke bush, magnolia, laurel and indeed, the foliage of many common trees and shrubs can be preserved by this method. There are just a couple of points to note before embarking on the process for yourself. Always use fresh-cut branches and stems, which absorb the glycerine mixture more quickly and efficiently than old, half-dead material. Cut the stems when the sap is still rising, usually in the summer, and remove any damaged or new leaves before the glycerine reaches them as they don't respond well to it. Finally, a warning that this method can become surprisingly expensive. Start with just a few stems of foliage in a small container and see for yourself how much of the glycerine and water mix they absorb. Better by far to have one or two stems of perfectly preserved leaves than a bucketful of half-finished ones.

The wonderful thing about glycerined foliage is that it retains its suppleness, unlike flowers dried by other methods. Less pleasing, perhaps, is the change of colour that often results. Some foliage, particularly that with a naturally brown tint such as oak and copper beech, becomes a superb dark or bronzy brown, but green leaves may turn to a murky khaki and ivy occasionally yellows. To counteract this you can add a few drops of food colouring to the glycerine, which opens up all kinds of opportunities for unusual shades and variations.

To preserve individual large leaves or small sprays of leaves in glycerine, immerse them completely until their colour changes. Wash them in a mild detergent before using them in arrangements.

Desiccation

Another drying method which offers quite different results is desiccation. This is a time-consuming process best-suited to small quantities of flowers; I have rarely used it at Armscote because it is too labour intensive and expensive for use on a large scale. The process involves the use of a drying agent, usually silica gel, to absorb the water in the flowers and leave it perfectly dried. The results can be quite spectacular and it is possible to preserve both the colour and shape of delicate flowers such as tulips, lilies, orchids, anemones and daffodils almost perfectly. Other flowers, particularly the larger ones, suffer some discolouration, but are still useful for their dramatic size and form.

It would take time and dedication to dry sufficient quantities of flowers for a decent-sized arrangement. And because only the flower heads themselves are dried, one has to wire each of them up individually. I have seen air-dried arrangements featuring a few of these perfectly preserved flowers as a highlight, but can't personally recommend this approach. Neither type of material looked its best; the air-dried material seemed unduly dull and the desiccated flowers insubstantial and brittle against their robust background. However, desiccated flowers do look good when placed in bowls of potpourri or when arranged together to give an almost lifelike effect.

If you have the patience to try this method yourself you will need silica gel crystals. (Alum, borax and hot sand can all be used in the same way but take longer to work.) Silica crystals can be obtained from good florists' suppliers (see page 135) and from chemists. If there is a choice, buy the colour-indicator type. This will probably be a strong blue colour which will turn pink when it becomes moist, or white with blue grains which will change colour when they are damp. If necessary, grind the crystals in a food processor until they are the texture of fine-ground coffee. Take an airtight container – a biscuit tin or plastic food container is fine – and cover the base with a layer of the silica. Onto this place individual flower heads. They should not touch, so don't aim to pack in more than four or five medium-sized flowers.

Using an artist's paintbrush, ease the crystals between the petals. Slowly and carefully, so as not to distort the shape of the flowers, cover them completely with more of the silica. Seal the lid of the container and leave it for two days. When you open it after that time you may find that the crystals have changed colour. Excavate the flowers very gently using a slotted kitchen spoon. They should feel firm and dry. If they don't, put them back and test again the following day. Don't leave them longer than this before testing them because they will continue to dry out and will become increasingly brittle and difficult to handle. When they are dry, dust off any excess silica crystals using the paintbrush, and you should have a perfectly preserved and gorgeously-coloured flower to contribute to your arrangement. The silica crystals can be dried out in an oven and used for the next batch of flowers. Be very careful to keep these flowers in a warm, dry atmosphere, otherwise they may become limp and begin to wilt.

Some authorities suggest using this process for delphiniums, larkspur and roses, but personally I think these can be perfectly well air-dried. Air-dried roses may not look quite so lifelike in their bunches, but once steamed and opened individually they are superb. I would reserve the silica method for flowers that really can't be preserved in any other way.

If you have no immediate use for the flowers you have dried, store them in a cool, dry, airy place. They can be left hanging in their original bunches or put in boxes. Use newspaper or tissue paper to protect the flower heads and leave the top of the box open so that air can reach the material. Don't pack any flowers that are not completely dry – they may rot and ruin everything around them. Another potential storage problem worth mentioning is mice. Before you store your materials in a garage or shed, particularly in the country, make sure you don't have mice in there. They love dried flowers and can wreak absolute havoc with your precious materials.

Plants Suitable For Preserving With Glycerine

This list includes only those plants for which this method of preservation is the best option. Others, such as hydrangeas, may also be preserved in this way but are more easily air dried. This is by no means a comprehensive list, so don't feel nervous about experimenting with material from your garden.

Aspidistra leaves

Beech leaves

Bergenia

Box

Camellia leaves

Catkins

Chestnut leaves

Cotoneaster

Eleagnus

Eucalyptus leaves

Fatsia (preserve single leaves only)

Hypericum ferns

Ivy

Laurel leaves

Magnolia leaves

Mahonia

Mexican orange

Moluccella

Oak leaves

Rhododendron (preserve single leaves only)

Flowers Suitable For Desiccation

Almost all flowers are suited to this means of preservation, but it is most practical to concentrate on those delicate varieties that cannot be dried in any other way. Experiment and see what happens. If petals drop from flowers preserved in this way you can stick them back with a discreet spot of glue.

Anemone

Camellia

Carnations

Clematis

Cyclamen

Dahlia

Freesia

Gentian

Hellebore

Hyacinth

Iris

Lily flowers of all varieties

Marigold

Narcissus

Orchid

Pansy

Passion Flower

Poppy

Primrose

Rhododendron

Tulip

Violet

Wallflower

EQUIPMENT AND MATERIALS

The materials and implements used throughout this book are all obtainable from good florists' shops or suppliers (see page 135). To produce most of the arrangements one would need a basic kit consisting of:

Florists' scissors – strong, high-quality scissors for cutting plant stems and wires.

Stub/florists' wires – range in length from 3½-18 inches (9-37cm) and from fine to heavy gauge, 24 gauge to 18 gauge. The finer the gauge, the higher the number. Most professional florists use medium and heavy gauge wires, though they may be too tough for unskilled fingers to manipulate. The best length to begin with is around 9 inches (22.5cm).

Reel wire – comes in either silver or dark green. The dark green shows up less in arrangements. I recommend using 26 gauge.

Dry foam – looks similar to styrofoam, but is softer and holds flowers better. It can be bought in a variety of shapes and sizes. Unless you need a sphere or a cone, buy large blocks and cut them to size.

Carving/floral knife – or other long-bladed knife for cutting foam.

Other useful items of equipment include:

Florists' tape – narrow, shiny black on one side. It sticks well to dry foam and is useful for holding it in position.

Chicken wire – for creating a base for flowers. 1½ inch (3.5cm) gauge is the easiest to work with.

Gutta-percha/floral tape – a rubber-based tape used for winding around stem wires and concealing unattractive ends. It comes in a variety of shades.

Florists' spikes and dry foam fixative/setting clay – used together to secure dry foam to shallow bowls and other 'difficult' containers. A small piece of fixative/setting clay holds the spike to the container, and the dry foam is impaled on the spike. The fixative/setting clay can often be removed from glass and china containers without causing damage.

Glue – useful for sticking awkward flowers and materials to arrangements. Use fast-drying clear glue or, for stronger bonding, a glue gun.

Wreath rings and posy holders – useful commercially-available bases for wreaths and posies. They can save time and trouble and give neater results. Wire wreath rings are particularly useful because of their light weight.

SUPPLIERS OF DRIED FLOWERS

There are hundreds of dried-flower stockists all over the country. Look in the Yellow Pages directory under Florists and Florists' Supplies for an indication of those in your area. Many florists specify in their advertisements whether or not they sell dried flowers loose or arranged. It's also worth checking your local garden centre – an increasing number are offering dried material. Here are some further suggestions:

*All suppliers that are marked with this symbol stock Armscote Manor Dried Flowers' arrangements at the time of writing.

UK SUPPLIERS

In London:

Covent Garden Flower Market
New Covent Garden
London SW8
Tel: (01) 720 2211
The stockist I recommend here is Multiflora, which supplies many retailers and also sells flowers to the public – though you may have to buy some things in bulk rather than in individual bunches. They carry a comprehensive and ever-changing range of stock. If you plan to visit Covent Garden, go early. By 7.30-8 a.m. the market is beginning to close down.

James Bodenham & Co*
89 Jermyn Street
London SW1
Tel: (01) 930 5340

Chattels
53 Chalk Farm Road
London NW1
Tel: (01) 267 0877

Fenwicks of Bond Street*
63 New Bond Street
London W1
Tel: (01) 629 9161

General Trading Company
144 Sloane Street
London SW1
Tel: (01) 730 0411

Graham and Green*
4-7 Elgin Crescent
London W11
Tel: (01) 727 4594

Harrods Ltd*
Knightsbridge
London SW1
Tel: (01) 730 1234

Heal & Son Ltd
196 Tottenham Court Road
London W1
Tel: (01) 636 1666

Camilla Hepper*
296 Chiswick High Road
London W4
Tel: (01) 995 2293

Hillier & Hilton
98 Church Road
London SW13
Tel: (01) 748 1810

Longmans Florists*
Selfridges Ltd
Oxford Street
London W1
Tel: (01) 629 1234

and

46 Holborn Viaduct*
London EC1
Tel: (01) 583 1440

Westminster Cathedral Shop*
42 Francis St
London SW1
Tel: (01) 828 4962

The following two florists sell or can be commissioned to make arrangements of the very highest quality:

Robert Day Flowers
89 Pimlico Road
London SW1
Tel: (01) 824 8655

Kenneth Turner Flowers
35 Brook Street
London W1
Tel: (01) 629 7837

Stores with branches around the country selling loose dried flowers and/or arrangements include:

Boots*
Habitat – who also have a good variety of containers.
Homebase*
Lewis's*
Makro*
The National Trust*
Next
Perrings*

The following shops, listed alphabetically according to town or city, stock dried flowers and/or dried-flower arrangements. If you have precise requirements, telephone first and find out whether they can supply you.

Nova
20 Chapel Street
Aberdeen AB1 15P
Tel: (0224) 641270

Spats
97 Groomsport Road
Bangor
Northern Ireland
Tel: (0247) 453264

Talbot Gray Ltd
26 Horsemarket
Barnard Castle
County Durham DL12 8LZ
Tel: (0833) 38072

Temptation
211 High Street
Berkhamsted
Hertfordshire HP4 1AD
Tel: (0442) 874333

The Molescraft Garden Centre
114 Woodhall Way
Beverley
Yorkshire
Tel: (0482) 881172

China Plus
148 High Street
Chipping Ongar
Essex
Tel: (0277) 656178

Artworks
The Watershed
Canons Road
Bristol BS1 5UN
Tel: (0272) 294803

Trevor Edwards Garden Centre
Scotch Quarter
Carrickfergus
County Antrim
Northern Ireland
Tel: (09603) 51123

Grosvenor Garden Centre
Wrexham Road
Belgrave
Chester CH4 9EB
Tel: (0244) 682856

Dixon & Co
Church Street
Coleraine BT52 1A4
Northern Ireland
Tel: (0265) 42076

The Thursday Shop
52 Finkle Street
Cottingham
North Humberside HU16 4A2
Tel: (0482) 844921

The Dartington Trading Co. Ltd
Shinners Bridge
Dartington
Devon TQ9 6TQ
Tel: (0803) 864171

The Old Stockhouse
60 West Street
Dorking
Surrey RH4 1BS
Tel: (0306) 882783

Casa Fina
107 Hanover Street
Edinburgh EH1 2DJ
Tel: (031) 225 2442

Jenners
48 Princes Street
Edinburgh EH2 2YJ
Tel: (031) 225 2442

Ditman and Malpass
9 West Street
Havant
Hampshire DO9 1EN
Tel: (0705) 483047

First Base
11 Silver Walk
St Martins Square
Leicester LE1 5EW
Tel: (0533) 629215

Jasmin
Holly Court
118 High Street
Midsomer Norton
Avon BA3 2DL
Tel: (0761) 419202

Country Choice
2 Blenheim Road
Minehead
Somerset TA24 5PY
Tel: (0643) 706584

Barkers
198-202 High Street
Northallerton
North Yorkshire DL7 8LP
Tel: (0609) 772303

Hovells
Bridewell Alley
Norwich NR2 1AE
Tel: (0603) 626676

Campion
26 High Street
Uppermill
Oldham
Lancashire
Tel: (0457) 876341

Pickwick Papers
The Gallery
90 Gloucester Green
Oxford OX1 2BU
Tel: (0865) 793149

J.R. Taylor
4-12 Garden Street
St Annes-on-Sea
Lancashire FY8 2AB
Tel: (0253) 722266

Clouds of Swansea
Unit 8
St David's Centre
Swansea SA1 3LE
Tel: (0792) 648093

Armscote Manor Dried Flowers
Armscote
Near Stratford-upon-Avon
Warwickshire CV37 8DA
Tel: (060882) 681

Mc'Illroy's
64-72 Regent Street
Swindon
Wiltshire SN1 1JX
Tel: (0793) 619487

US SUPPLIERS

Arrowhead Gardens
115 Boston Post Road
Wayland, MA 01778
Tel: (508) 358-7333

Bachman's Inc
6010 Lyndale Avenue South
Minneapolis, MN 55419
Tel: (612) 861-7600

W. Atlee Burpee Co
300 Park Avenue
Warminster, PA 18974
Tel: (215) 674-4900

Carroll Gardens
P.O. Box 310
Westminster, MD 21157
Tel: (301) 848-5422
(Sell flower-drying kits)

Emlong Nurseries
2671 West Marquette Woods Road
Stevensville, MI 49127
Tel: (616) 429-3431

Farmer Seed and Nursery
818 Northwest 4th Street
Faribault, MN 55021
Tel: (507) 334-1625

Earl Ferris Nursery
811 4th Street, NE
Hampton, IA 50441
Tel: (515) 456 2563

Sjulin's Swedish Touch
RR2, Box 2
Hamburg, IA 51640
Tel: (712) 382-2383

Jung Seed Co
335 South High Street
Randolph, WI 53957
Tel: (414) 326-3121

Keil Brothers
220-15 Horace Harding Blvd.
Bayside, NY 11364
Tel: (718) 224-2020

Moon Mountain Wildflowers
P.O. Box 34
Morro Bay, CA 93442
Tel: (805) 772-2473

L.L. Olds Seeds Co
2901 Packers Avenue
Madison, WI 53704
Tel: (608) 249-9291

Putney Nursery
Box 265
Putney, VT 05340
Tel: (802) 387-5577

Scarff's Nursery
Route 1
Carlisle, OH 45344
Tel: (513) 845-3130

People's Flower Corporation
786 6th Avenue
New York, NY 10001
Tel: (212) 686-6291

Rialto Florist, Inc
707 Lexington Ave
New York, NY 10022
Tel: (212) 688-3204

Richard Salome Flowers
152 East 79th St
New York, NY 10021
Tel: (212) 988-2933

Smith & Hawken
23 Corte Madera
Mill Valley, CA 94941
Tel: (415) 383-4050

Galerie Felix Flower
968 Lexington Ave
New York, NY 10021
Tel: (212) 772-7701

Gardener's Eden
Williams Sonoma
P.O. Box 7307
San Francisco, CA 91120
Tel: (415) 421-4242

The following suppliers ship dried plants to order:

Catnip Acres Herb Nursery
67 Christian Street
Oxford, Connecticut 06483
Tel: (203) 885-5649
(Dried flowers and herbs. Seed catalogue $2.)

Stamens & Pistils
875 Third Avenue
New York, NY 10022
Tel: (212) 593-1888
(Dried tropical flowers and foliage. No catalogue.)

Sura Kayla
484 Broome Street
New York, NY 10013
Tel: (212) 941-8757
(Dried flowers and grasses. For brochure send SASE.)

Tom Thumb Workshop
Route 13
P.O. Box 357
Mappsville, VA 23407
Tel: (804) 824-3507
(Dried flowers and herbs. Catalogue $1.)

Wayside Gardens
1 Garden Lane
Hodges, SC 29695-0001
Tel: (800) 845-1124
(Dried flowers. Free catalogue.)

Well-Sweep Herb Farm
317 Mount Bethel Road
Port Murray, NJ 07865
Tel: (201) 852-5390
(Dried flowers and herbs. Catalogue $1.)

A PLANT LEXICON

Identifying plants can be a confusing business. All have Latin names, which it can be useful to know when ordering flowers from suppliers or buying seed to grow in the garden. Many plants are known by the abbreviated version of the Latin name, for example, *Alchemilla mollis* is usually known as alchemilla – and, then again, it's sometimes called by its traditional name, Lady's mantle. To complicate things further not all authorities agree on all the names. Where there is doubt, I have used the name by which we buy and sell the flowers at Armscote Manor.

In the table below I have listed the names of the most commonly available dried flowers. There simply isn't space to list every one of the different varieties of some species – one could write a short book on the different banksias and proteas alone – so I suggest you visit or contact suppliers in order to see for yourself what they have on offer.

Those plants which can fairly easily be grown in temperate climates and will make an attractive contribution to the flowerbeds I have marked with this symbol*. If you live in an area with a more extreme climate, consult an appropriate gardening book.

Latin Name	Common Name	Traditional Name
Acacia sp.	Mimosa/wattle	
Acanthus spinosus *	Acanthus	Bear's breeches
Achillea filipendulina *	Achillea	Yarrow
Achillea millefolium *	Lilac achillea	Yarrow
Achillea ptarmica	Achillea ptarmica	The Pearl/Pearl Achillea
Aconitum napellus *	Aconitum	Monkshood
Agapanthus africanus *	Agapanthus (seed heads)	
Agonis sp.	Titree	
Agrostis nebulosa	Cloud grass	
Alchemilla mollis *	Alchemilla	Lady's mantle
Allium sp.*	Onion	
Amaranthus sp.*	Amaranthus	Love-lies-bleeding/Prince's feathers
Ambrosinia sp.	Ambrosinia	
Ammobium alatum *	Sandflower	Winged flower
Anaphalis sp.*	Pearl everlasting	
Anethum graveolens *	Dill	
Anigozanthos sp.	Kangaroo paw	
Aphyllanthes sp.	Glixia	Grass daisy
Arctosis sp.	African daisy	
Artemisia vulgaris *	Artemisia	Mugwort
Arundinaria sp.*	Bamboo	
Astilbe davidii *	Astilbe	
Avena compacta *	Oats	
Banksia sp.	Banksia	Australian honeysuckle
Bergenia sp.*	Bergenia	Elephant's ear
Betula pendula	Silver birch	
Botao branco	Botao	Button flower
Briza maxima *	Large quaking grass	Pearl grass
Briza media *	Common quaking grass	
Briza minima *	Lesser quaking grass	
Briza segromi	Briza segromi	
Bromus formus	Bromus	Spear grass
Bupleurum sp.	Bupleurum	Gloss eyes
Buxifolium sp.	Buxifolium	
Calendula officinalis *	Pot marigold	
Callistemon beaufortia sparsa *	Red bottlebrush	
Capucin sp.	Capucin	
Carex sp.	Sedge	Bell reed
Carlina acaulis *	Stemless thistle	
Carthamus tinctorius *	Carthamus	Safflower or saffron thistle
Caspium limonium *	Caspia	
Caustus sp.	Caustus	Chinese puzzle
Celosia argentea cristata	Celosia	Cockscomb
Centaurea cyanus *	Cornflower	
Choisya ternata *	Choisya	Mexican orange blossom
Chrysanthemum sp.*	Chrysanthemum	
Chrysanthemum vulgare *	Tansy	
Cladonia sp.	Lichen	Reindeer or staghorn moss
Clematis vitalba *	Wild clematis	Old man's beard, Travellers' joy
Cortaderia selloana *	Pampas grass	
Craspedia globosa *	Craspedia	Drumstick plant
Cynara scolymus *	Globe artichoke	

*Dahlia**	Pompon dahlia	
*Delphinium consolida**	Larkspur	
Delphinium sp.*	Delphinium	
Dryandra formosa	Dryandra	
*Dryopteris filix-mas**	Male fern	
Dudinea sp.	Dudinea	
*Dumosa limonium iertericum**	Statice dumosa	Sea Lavender
*Echinops ritro**	Miniature thistle	
*Echinops bannaticus**	Globe thistle	
*Erica cinerea**	Bell heather	
*Eryngium planum**	Sea holly	
Eucalyptus sp.	Eucalyptus	Gum
*Fagus sylvatica**	Beech	
Fagus sylvatica 'Cuprea'*	Copper beech	
*Gomphrena globosa**	Globe amaranth	Spanish clover
Gossypium herbaceum	Cotton	
Grimmia pulvinata	Bun moss	
Gypsophila sp.*	Gypsophila	Baby's breath
Gypsophila rugosa	Broom bloom	
Hakea cucallata	Hakea	
*Hedera helix**	Ivy	
*Helichrysum angustifolium**	Curry plant	Stinking helichrysum
*Helichrysum bracteatum**	Helichrysum	Everlasting flower/ strawflower
*Helichrysum cordatum**	Seacrest	
*Helichrysum sesamoides**	Helichrysum	Everlasting flower
Helichrysum vestitum	Capblumen	
Helipterum manglesii	Rhodante	
Helipterum sanfordii	Cluster-flowered everlasting	
Helipterum sp.*	Acroclinium	
Helipterum subufolium	Helipterum	Sunray
Hordeum vulgare	Barley	
*Humulus lupulus**	Hop	
*Hydrangea macrophylla**	Hydrangea	
*Hydrangea paniculata**	Panicled hydrangea	
Hypericum sp.	Hypericum	St John's wort
Ixodia sp.	South Australian daisy	Australian daisy
Ixodia achilleoides	Immortelle	
Juncus sp.	Rush	
Kunzea sp.	Kunzea	
Lachnostachys sp.	Lachnostachys	
*Lagurus ovatus**	Lagurus	Hare's-tail grass/ bunny tails
Larix sp.	Larch cone	
*Lavandula spica**	Lavender	
Lepidium rurale (also known as *Lupidium*)	Lepidium	
Leptospermum sp.	Silver strawberry	
Leucodendron sp.	Leucodendron	
Liatris sp.*	Liatris	Blazing star/button snakeroot
*Limonium sinuatum**	Statice	
*Limonium suworowii**	Russian statice	Rat's tail statice/ Pink pokers
Lonas indora	Lonas	Small-headed achillea
*Lunaria annua**	Honesty	
Melaleuca sp.	Melaleuca or Brunia	
*Moluccella laevis**	Bells of Ireland	Shell flower
Nelumbo lucifera	Lotus flower heads	
Nervosum verticor	Nervosum	
*Nigella damascena**	Nigella	Love-in-a-mist
Nigella orientalis	Nigella orientalis	
*Paeonia lactiflora**	Peony	
*Papaver rhoeas**	Poppy (seed head)	
*Phalaris arundinacea**	Canary grass	
Phleum sp.	Timothy grass	Rats' tails
*Phlomis fruticosa**	Jerusalem sage	
Phragmites australis	Reed	
*Physalis alkekengi franchetti**	Physalis	Chinese lantern
Pinus sp.	Pine cone	
*Pithocarpa corymbulosa**	Miniature everlasting	
Polypogon sp.	Polypogon	Hare's-foot grass
Protea sp.	Protea	Cape honey flower
*Pyrus salicifolia**	Weeping pear	
Ranunculus sp.*	Buttercup	
Rosa sp.*	Rose	
Rumex sp.*	Dock or sorrel	
Ruscus sp.	Ruscus	
*Salvia farinacea**	Blue salvia	
*Senecio greyi**	Senecio	
*Silene pendula**	Silene	Campion
Solidago sp.*	Golden rod	
Solidaster sp.	Solidaster	
Sphagnum sp.	Sphagnum moss	
*Stachys lanata**	Lamb's tongue	
*Stirlingia latifolia**	Stirlingia	
Triticum sp.	Wheat	
Typha sp.	Reedmace	
Verticordia brownii	Verticordia	
Verticordia ruitens	Morrison or feather flower	
Xeranthemum sp.	Silver everlasting flower	
Zea mays	Sweet corn	Maize
Zinnia sp.*	Zinnia	

INDEX

A

acanthus 75, 140
accessories: birds' nests 42, 100
    coral fans 67
    for Easter theme 96, 100
        making chicks 100
    kitchen implements 24, *24*
    musical instruments 42
    paper ribbon 56
    shells 62
    sponges/loofahs *66*, 67
    statuary 42
    stones 45
achillea 27, 72, 75, 79, 90, 96, 104, 108, 112,
    140
acorns 23, 45
agapanthus 45, 140
air drying 73
    methods 130-1
alchemilla 29, 30, 32, 46, *46*, 48, 53, 58, 60,
    72, 75, *75*, 80, 96, 108, 112, 114, 140
Allium siculum 75, 140
alstroemeria 75
    fresh 111
altar rails *85*, 87
amaranthus 27, 30, 32, 36, 46, 56, 60, 67,
    104, 118, 140
ambrosinia 68, 140
arrangements: for beginners 96
    cheapest/simplest 101
    for children 96, 100
    for church, fixing 79-80, 86
    country house style 32ff.
    country-style *27*, 27-9
        bunches *85*
    floor-standing 58
    gauging proportions 103
    hanging 29, 64, *71*, 72
    Indian-inspired 60-2, *61*
    individual 37
    for large/awkward spaces 82-3, *85*
    linking house and garden 64
    low 46-7, 100
    measuring space for 46
    modern continental 62-3
    multiples *56*, 58, *97*
        adding contrast to 104
    narrow/flat-backed *see* Becher's Brook
    photographing stages of 90
    practicality of dried 86
    rustic 108, *109*
    small-scale 96, *97*
    symmetrical 64
    three rules for 27

    traditional 37-41
    trailing *45*, 46, 55, *55*
    year-round 35, 100, 108-12, *110*, *112*, 122
        advantages of 111
        instructions for making 114-16
artichokes 72, 104, 140
    drying method 75, 130

B

Banksia baxteri 62, *62*, 140
banksias 29, 32, 140
barley 29, 141
bathrooms 64-7, *66*
baubles, Christmas 118, 124
bay 22
Becher's Brook 24-6, *25*
    instructions for making 30-1
bedrooms 27, *46*, 46ff., *52*
    fantasy *52*, 52-3
beech leaves 42, 92, *92*, 104
    glycerined 87
borage 22
botao 'buttons' 53, 58, *59*, 60, 64, 80, 96, 140
bouquet garnis 22-3
bows: for bridal bouquet 92
    for bridal headdress 92
    Christmas 117, 118, 124
    flower-covered 79
    wired *85*, 87, *87*, 92
bracken 32, 46, 101, 104, 111
bread, freshly baked 23-4, *24*, 108
    preserving 24
brambles, fruiting 37
bridal bouquet 92, *92*
bridal headdress 92
Briza segromi 64, 140
broom bloom 60, 62, 101, 104, 108, 141
bulrushes 45, 46
bunches, wiring 118
buttercups 72, 75, *75*

C

capucin leaves 36, 62, 140
carline thistle 75, 140
carthamus 23, 32, 46, 64, 67, 75, 96, 140
catmint 22, 72
caustus 45, 82, 140
ceiling beams 29
celosia 37, 48, 62, 79, 87, 92, 104, 140
chairs 111
chest of drawers *43*, 45
chicken wire 92
    shaping 58
        for garland 90
Chinese lanterns 32, *32*, 104, 108, 111, 112,

    124
chives 22
choir stalls 90
Christmas 117ff.
Christmas presents 124, *124*
Christmas tree 48, 120, *120*
    instructions for making 126-7
chrysanthemums, fresh spray 111, 140
cinnamon sticks 48, 60
    as lining material 55
    wiring in bundles 118
coconuts 60
colours: autumn tints 101, 103-4, *104*
    choice for large trees 64
    for Christmas 117
    cool *52*, 52-3, 104
    'difficult' *53*
    difficulties in co-ordinating 35-6
    light *52*, 52-3
    limiting shades *28*
    making swatches 30, 46, 87
    muted 87, 104
    using colour spectrum 104
    using contrasts 35, 46, 103, 104
    warm 32, *32*, 37-42
cones: on Christmas presents 124, *124*
    fir 45, 92, 124, 141
        gold-sprayed 124
        wiring 118
    larch 23, 141
    perfumed 122
containers 101, 108
    barrels 103-4, *104*
    baskets 22, 30, 62, 111-12, *112*
    boxes 53, 62, 75
    breadcrocks 23, *24*
    buckets *71*, 72
    cachepots *56*, 56-7
    candelabra 42
    chamber-pot *66*, 67
    chinaware 96
    choosing 27
    copper pans 27, *27*
    flowerpots 23, *23*, 29, 37, 68
    glass 36, 55, *55*, 56, *56*
        linings for 36, *46*, 55
    importance of 67
    jugs 53, *66*, 96, *97*
    lining 62
    sack 101
    silverware 36
    for table decorations 111
corn cobs 64, 111, 140
    see also maize

cornflowers 72, 140
cotton 60, 141
cow parsley 72
craspedia 46, 140
Craspedia globosa 101, 140
cupboards 29, *29*
curry plant 22, 141

D

daffodils 130
dahlias 30, 32, *32*, 104, 141
daisies 53, 101, *110*, 140
    African 90, 108
    brown-eyed 60
    tree, instructions for making 68-9
delphiniums 37, 53, 72, 101, 112, 141
desiccation drying method 132
    plants suitable for 133
dining-rooms 32-5, *35*
dining-table 27, 37, 100, 108, *110*, 111
    see also chairs
dock 60, 104, 141
doors/doorways 29, 64, 82, 118
    for weddings 79-80, *80*
        church porch 79, 79-80
drawing-room 27
dressing table 48, *49*
dryandra 62, 141
drying methods 22, 72-3, 130
    see also individual methods
dudinea 29, 32, 36, 141
dust/dusting 46

E

Easter celebration 96ff.
equipment list 134
eryngium 72, 141
eucalyptus: leaves 87, 96, 104, 141
    glycerined 92, *92*
    seeds 45

F

ferns 42, 82, 90, 118
feverfew 22
fireplace 58, 120, *120*
fixatives 118
flax 27, 36, 58, 60, 96
florists' tape, using 23, 36, 58, 67
florists' vials 111
florists' wire 22
foam: fixing in glass containers 36
    for trees 48
foliage 42, 68
    re-cycling 55
    see also individual types
fresh flowers 100
    see also arrangements, year-round
fruit, fresh 37, 80, *80*

apples 101
    baskets of 122
    lining container for 62
    oranges/satsumas 117, 118, *118*, 124
        wiring 118
    strawberries/raspberries 112, *112*
    technique for attaching 22
fungi, dried 45

G

garlands 48, *49*
    around basket 45
    around pot rims 68
    Christmas *122*, 122-4
        reworking *122*
    as curtain tie-backs 53
    decorating 111
    flower 37
    with fruit 37
    garlic 22, 104, *104*
    hay *108*
        instructions for making 108
    measuring for 82, 90
    moss 23, 67, 79, 111
        fixing 23
    rope *85*, 118
        instructions for making 82-3
    on staircases 82
    wedding *79*, 79-80, *80*, *85*, *87*, 87-8, 92
garlic 22, 104, *104*
gazebo 82
glixia 30, 32, 53, 56, 58, 64, 80, 96, 124, 140
    sprayed with metallic paint 64
globe amaranth 75, 141
globe thistles 55, 67, 75, 141
glycerine, preserving with 42' 131
    plants suitable for 133
gomphrenas 112, 140
grasses 27, 53
    quaking 27, 32, 48, 87, 140
gypsophila 32, 53, 58, 64, 80, 86, 96, 124, 141

H

hallways/passages 24-6, *25*
harvest festival 101ff.
heather 111
hedgerow/wild flowers 27, 62, 101
    used outdoors 72
Helichrysum vestitum capblumen 53, 141
helichrysums 27, 48, 58, 62, 72, 80, 87, 90, 96, 103-4, 108, *110*, 111, 124, 141
Helipterum sanfordii 96, 141
helipterums 68, 100, 141
herbs, dried 22, *23*
    gathering 22, *23*
honesty 72, 80, 141
    green 27, 75, *75*
    miniature variety 80

honeysuckle, Australian 32
hop bine 29
hoya leaves 87
hyacinths 100
hydrangeas 30, 37, 58, 60, 72, 79, 82, 111, 141
    trees 64

I

immortellum 96, 141
ivy: glycerined 37, 42, 45, 92
    trailing 118

K

kangaroo paw 42, 46, 140
kitchens 22ff., 27ff.
kunzea 48, 118, 141
    as basic foliage 126

L

larkspur 30, 36, 48, 53, 56, 60, 72, 79, 80, 86, 90, 96, 108, 111, 114
    stalks 48
lavender 22, 36, 56, 60, 67, 75, 82, 96, 101, 111, 141
    as lining material 36, 55
    potpourri 48, 55, *55*
leek heads 72, 75, *75*
leptospermum 36, 141
lichen 42, 140
    drying method 130
    for headdresses 92
    as lining material 55
licorice sticks 60
Limonium suworowii 101, 141
living-rooms 32, *32*
    difficult corners in 62, *62*
lotus seed pods 60, *61*, 79, *80*, 141
lupidium 68, 87, 90

M

magnolia leaves, skeletal 92, *92*
mahonia 42
maize, drying method 130, 140
mantelpiece *56*, 56-7
marjoram 22, 72
materials: collecting samples 87
    continuity of 48
    exotic 60, *61*, 62
    'expendable' 72
    gathering for drying 72-3
    good fillers 72
    growing your own 72
    judging quantities 92
    for large trees 64
    list of 134
    for 'natural' theme 101
    for outdoors *71*, 72ff.
    storing 124
    for year-round arrangement 111

midsummer night celebration 111-12, *112*
mimosa 29, 37, 79, 80, 111, 140
mind-your-own-business *60*
miniature landscape *43*, 45
moss: balls of 100
    bun 48
    drying method 130
    mixing different 45
    trees of 48
    with roses 64
    as trimming 101, 124
    reindeer 90, 92
    Spanish 53
        as lining material 55, 68
    sphagnum 36, 68, 103, 141
    for rope garland 82

N

narcissi, fresh 100
Nervosum verticor 29, 141
nigella 29, 36, *46*, 48, 53, 72, 87, 90, 108, 114, 141
Nigella orientalis 56, 58, 141
nutmegs 60, *61*
nuts 23, 45
    almonds 60
    chestnuts 23
    lining container for 62
    walnuts 122

O

oak leaves 45, 104, 118
oats 27, 29, 32, 53, 87, 96, 101, 104, *110*, 111, 140
    sheaf of 79, *80*
onion heads, drying method 130

P

palm: berries 62
    spears 62, *62*
pampas grass 46, 140
Paranomus sphathulatus 64
pelmets 53
peonies 36, 37, 58, 60, *60*, 72, 75, 86, 141
    steaming open 60
Peruvian lily 75
pews *90*, 92
phalaris 96, 101, 108, 141
Phylica rigida 42, 62
piano 42, 45
picture frames 82
pink poker 101, 141
plant lexicon 140-1
polyanthus, fresh 100
pomanders 45, 48
    Christmas 117
        instructions for making 122
    making flower-covered 64

perfumed 64, *66*
poplar leaves, glycerined 90
poppadums 60, *61*
poppies 75, 141
    heads 53, 75, 90, 101, 104, *104*, 111, 124
        making clusters of 118
posy, lace-edged 48, *49*
potpourri 48, *49*
    lining containers with 36, *46*, 55, 68
Protea sulphurea 23, 92, *92*, 141
proteas 62, *62*, 111, 141
pulpit *90*

Q

Queen Anne's lace 72

R

radiator screens 45
reception-room 56
reeds *52*, 52-3
rice 60
root ginger, dried 60
rosemary 22
roses 30, 36, 46, *46*, 47, 56, 58, 60, *60*, 67, 72, 75, 79, 82, 86, 87, 90, 92, *92*, 96, 104, 111-12
    miniature 92
    petals 56
    rambling 87
    spray 101
    steaming open 60
    trees of 64

S

sage 22
screen, church 90
seacrest 52, 55, *55*, 87, 92, 141
sea holly 29, 141
sea lavender 53, 72, 86, 87, 108, *110*, 111, 114, 124, 141
    as background material 117-18
        for Christmas tree 126
seed pods 62
    see also individual types
settings: rustic 62, *62*
    sketching 46
shelves, high 45
silica gel crystals 124, 132
silver strawberry 36
smoke tree 42, 75
Soleirolia soleirolii 60
spices 60
    mixture for 'curing' pomander 122
staircases 27, *27*, 82
stalks: bamboo 60, *61*
    in bouquet 92
    re-cycling 55
statice 46, 53, 58, 72, 79, 90, 111, 141
    Russian 27, 141

stirlingia 92
strelitzia 92
suppliers 135-9
sweet peas, fresh 112
swing 53

T

tamarinds 60
    husks 23
tansy 22
titree 42, 56, 64, 79
tomatoes, dried 60
trees, fantasy 23, 48, *49*, 60
    Christmas 120
    daisy, instructions for making 68-9
    foliage for 68
    large 64, *64*
    refreshing material on 68
twigs/branches 23
    apple 23, 68, 101
        flowering 100
    banana 22, 42
    blue spruce 118
    cane 92
    with catkins 100
    cherry, flowering 100
    contorted willow 52, *52*
    florentine 64
    holly 118, 122
    lime 92
    as trimming 30
    yew 118, *112*

U

utility rooms 22

V

vegetables: dried 72
    technique for attaching 22
verticordia 29, 58, 60, 62, 104, *104*, 118, 141
vestitum 53

W

wardrobe *45*, 45-6
weddings 79ff.
    winter *85*, 86ff.
weeping pear 42, 87
wheat 24, 108, *110*, 111
    sheaf 101
        instructions for making *103*
        in varying sizes 111
windowsill 53, *53*
wreaths: Christmas 120
    construction of 117-18
    harvest festival 101
    small cane 124
    wall 58-60, *59*
    wedding 79
        apple-covered 80, *80*

Egypt

Alasdair Tenquist

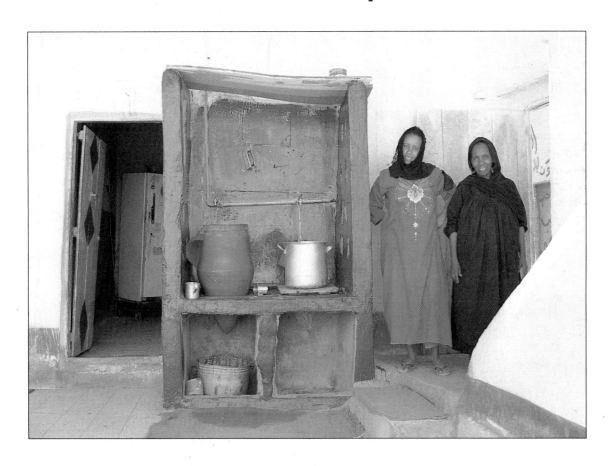

Wayland

Economically Developing Countries

Bangladesh	**India**
Brazil	**Mexico**
China	**Nigeria**
Egypt	**Peru**
Ghana	**Vietnam**

Cover picture: A busy open-air vegetable market in Cairo.
Title page: Nubian women from Egypt's south.
Contents page: The camel market at Imbaba in Cairo.

Picture acknowledgements: All photographs are by James H. Morris, except:
Associated Press 32 (top),35; Camera Press 32 (bottom); Topham Picture Source 5
(bottom), 34; Wayland Picture Library/Julia Waterlow 10, 31.

Series editor: Paul Mason
Book editor: Polly Goodman
Designer: Mark Whitchurch

First published in 1995 by
Wayland (Publishers) Ltd
61 Western Road, Hove
East Sussex, BN3 1JD, England

British Library Cataloguing in Publication Data
Tenquist Alasdair
    Egypt. - (Economically Developing
    Countries Series)
    I. Title II. Series
    916.2

ISBN 0 7502 1575 5

Typeset by Mark Whitchurch, England
Printed and bound by G.Canale & C.s.p.A. – Borgaro T.se – Turin, Italy

Contents

Introduction   4

Deserts and delta   7

The people of Egypt   13

In the city   19

In the countryside   25

Why is Egypt poor?   31

Development in Egypt   36

The future of Egypt   42

Glossary   46

Further information   47

Index   48

Introduction

Egypt is a country of contrasts and surprises. The first images that come to mind are of the pyramids, temples and cities of the ancient Egyptians. For over 5,000 years there has been civilization along the Nile, making it one of the oldest occupied places on earth. Yet the country we know as Egypt today was only formed in 1936, and nearly half of its people are under fifteen years old.

Similarly, there is a striking contrast in landscapes. Most of the country is a huge, empty desert – bare rock, sand or gravel where only a few people can scratch out a living. Yet along the green and fertile valley of the River Nile, people are crowded together in village after village, often eking out a difficult existence on tiny farms. Even more densely populated are the cities, where 80 per cent of the population now live. Here, amongst the chaos and the noise, the super-rich sit in stretch Mercedes, jostling for position in endless traffic jams, next to the ramshackle taxis, donkeys and bare feet of the city's poor.

'About Egypt I will have a great deal more to relate, because of the number of remarkable things that the country contains.'
– Herodotus, Greek historian and traveller (484–424 BC).

A busy street in the markets of Old Cairo.

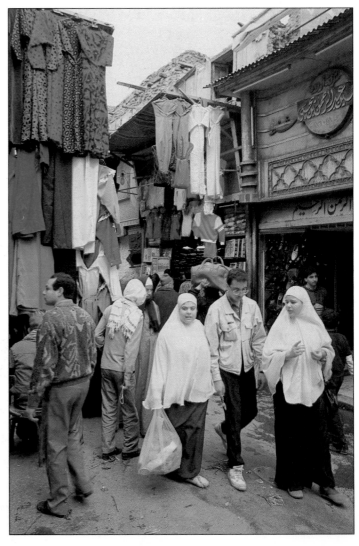

ORIGIN OF THE NAME 'EGYPT'

The English word 'Egypt' comes from the ancient Egyptian *Het-ka-ptah*. 'Ka' means the soul and *'ptah'* is a god. When the Greeks arrived they changed this to *Ai-gy-ptious*, from which we get Egypt.

Egypt's official name is the Arab Republic of Egypt, or in Egyptian Arabic, *Jumhuriyat Misr al-Arabiya*.

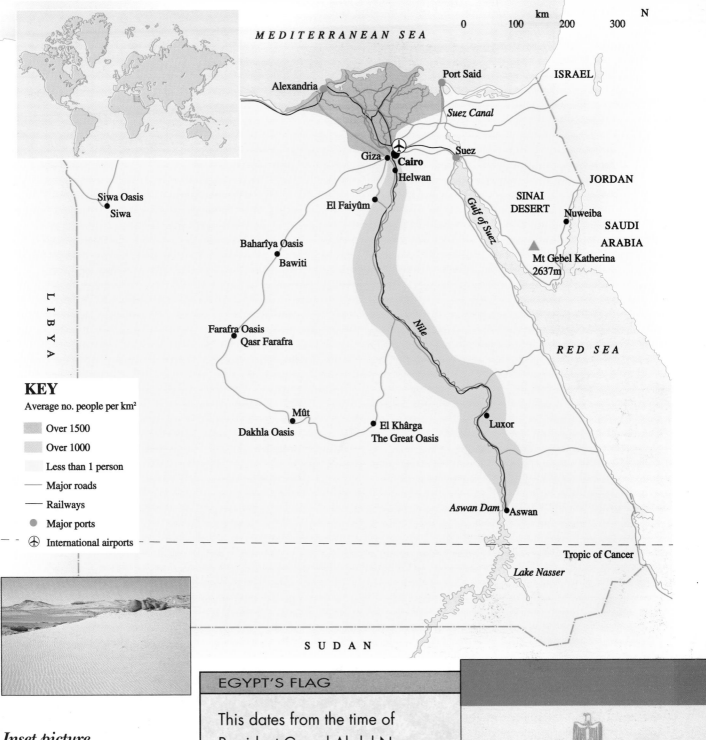

MEDITERRANEAN SEA

Port Said

ISRAEL

Alexandria

Suez Canal

Giza ✈ Cairo   Suez

Helwan

El Faiyûm

JORDAN

SINAI
DESERT

Siwa Oasis
Siwa

Nuweiba

SAUDI
ARABIA

Baharîya Oasis
Bawiti

▲ Mt Gebel Katherina
2637m

L
I
B
Y
A

Farafra Oasis
Qasr Farafra

Nile

Gulf of Suez

RED SEA

KEY

Average no. people per km²

Over 1500

Over 1000

Less than 1 person

Major roads

Railways

● Major ports

✈ International airports

Mût
Dakhla Oasis

El Khârga
The Great Oasis

Luxor

Aswan Dam ● Aswan

Tropic of Cancer

Lake Nasser

SUDAN

Inset picture
Sand dunes and
vast stretches of
barren desert make
up most of Egypt's
landscape.

EGYPT'S FLAG

This dates from the time of
President Gamal Abdel Nasser
(1954–1970). Nasser wanted
to stress Egypt's unity with the
rest of the Arab world by
adopting a flag popular in these states. The red symbolizes the
desert areas and the black the fertile Nile valley and delta.
Egypt's flag is different from the other Arab states in that it has
an eagle in the middle of the white band.

Egypt is without doubt one of the most fascinating and beautiful countries in the world, stocked with many rich resources. However, it also faces many problems. Above all, it has one of the world's fastest growing populations. Every month, another 1 million Egyptian babies are born, all needing food, clean water, housing, health care and other services that the Egyptian government cannot afford to provide. Their parents have to fight for the few jobs that are available so that they can provide food and shelter for their family. The alternative is a life on the streets. Many families have to survive on the equivalent of just US$1 a day.

Below left
Life in the deserts: wandering nomads.

Below Life in the cities on the streets: the homeless of Cairo sleep where they can.

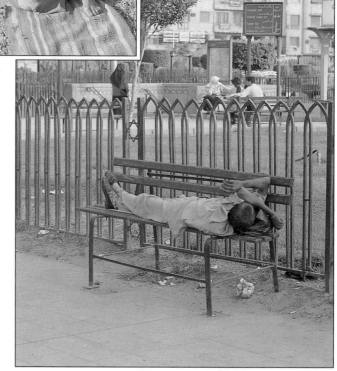

EGYPT AT A GLANCE	
Population:	60 million (1994 estimate.)
Capital:	Cairo (population 16 million)
Area:	1,001,449 km²
Currency:	Egyptian pound (E£), divided into 100 piastres.
Language:	Egyptian Arabic
Religon:	Islam
Foundation:	1936
President:	Hosni Mubarek
Constitution:	Democratic

Deserts and delta

Egypt's natural features.

Egypt is located in the north-eastern corner of the continent of Africa, and is crossed in the south by the Tropic of Cancer. It is bordered to the north by the Mediterranean Sea and to the east by the Red Sea. To the west are Libya and the vast bare wastes of the Sahara Desert.

LANDSCAPE

Egypt is a large country, yet 97 per cent of its surface cannot support human life. These are the 'red' lands, the desert areas outside the Nile valley, so called because of the

LANDSCAPE AND CLIMATE	
Highest point:	Gebel Katherina, 2,637 m above sea level.
Lowest point:	Qattâra Depression, 133 m below sea level.
Wettest place:	Alexandria (average annual rainfall 180 mm)
Driest place:	Aswân (1 mm per year)
Largest oasis:	Dâkhla, with 12,000 hectares of farmland.
Hottest place:	Aswân (average 40 °C)
Coolest place:	Alexandria (average 27 °C)

colour of the sand and rocks found there. The Sinai Peninsula sits between the main body of Egypt and Israel to the north-east. This is a dramatic, mountainous area, full of constantly changing shades of red, yellow and brown. The highest mountain in Egypt is here, at 2,637 metres. Between the River Nile and the Sinai are the Eastern Highlands, while to the west of the Nile is the Western Desert. It is this last area that best fits people's picture of a desert area, with vast areas of unbroken sand dunes. However, although there are many kilometres of dunes in the Western Desert, the majority of the area is not covered by sand at all, but rather 'regs' – coarse and barren gravel plains.

Football is played outside a village settled in the middle of vast gravel plains.

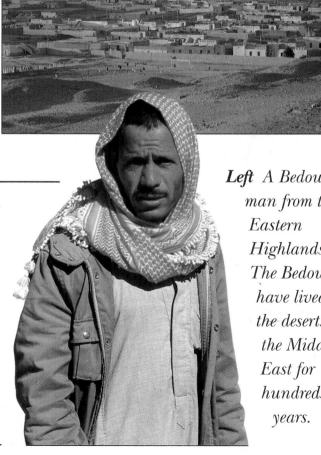

'We live close to the desert because it is our traditional way of life. You can only live in the desert if you understand it and have been brought up to live here. Increasing numbers of us work with tourists, since we can make more money this way.'
– Mohammed Gabr El Hakeem, of the Bisharin Bedouin people in the Eastern Highlands.

Left *A Bedouin man from the Eastern Highlands. The Bedouin have lived in the deserts of the Middle East for hundreds of years.*

The age-old feluccas are still the most popular form of transport on the Nile.

FELUCCAS

Despite the multi-million-dollar development going on around it, the easiest way for most people to travel on the Nile is by felucca. These are the traditional sailing boats, used since ancient times, to transport people, animals, goods and building materials up and down the nation's watercourses. It is said that the limestone blocks that were used to build the pyramids were carried in similar boats. For a small fee, usually bargained over a cup of tea, tourists are able to experience this ancient form of water transport. Most say it is the only way to really enjoy sunset over the Nile.

There are several parts of these dry areas of Egypt where the land actually drops well below sea level – these remain unfilled with water because there is so little rain in the desert. In fact, if a canal was dug from the sea to the lowest of these, the Qattâra Depression, the area would soon be filled with a lake 133 metres deep and 250 kilometres wide.

Running south to north through these deserts winds the floodplain and delta of the River Nile. Called the 'black' lands after its rich dark soils, this thin band of vegetation follows the River Nile from Lake Nasser on the border with Sudan until it empties into the Mediterranean Sea, some 1,600 kilometres further north.

After Cairo, the Nile divides into a delta. A delta is where a river fans out into two or more channels before it reaches the sea. The Nile delta is one of the world's largest, 250 kilometres wide at the Mediterranean Sea. If you were to travel in a boat through one of the many channels in the delta, you would be unlikely to see any wild countryside. Instead, just about every inch of the fertile ground is used for growing the food so desperately needed by the rapidly growing population.

Until the last century, no one could be sure of where the furthest source of the River Nile was. In the second century AD, Ptolemy, a famous Greek geographer, guessed that the true source was in the Mountains of the Moon, on the borders of Uganda and Zaire – an excellent guess as it turned out!

In the 1600s, Jesuit priests had discovered the source of the Blue Nile in Lake Tana in the Ethiopian Highlands. However, it was not until the nineteenth century that the source of the Nile was correctly identified as Lake Victoria in Uganda. Two Englishmen, Richard Burton and John Speke, set off in 1857 in search of the Nile's source. They survived malaria, the death of their pack animals and the mutiny of their porters before Burton fell seriously ill. Speke went on to discover Lake Victoria, which he later proved to be the Nile's source. Burton would not believe him and a great public debate was organized to settle the matter. The day before the debate, however, Speke died in a hunting accident. He never publicly heard that he was right.

The Nile is a 'seasonal' river: its level rises and falls with the seasons. In the past, Egyptian farmers would wait patiently each year for the rains to fall in the mountains of Ethiopia, one of the sources of the Nile. They knew that the river, swollen by these rains, would usually burst its banks when it reached the flat plains of Egypt. This allowed life-giving mud (silt) and water to settle across the valley floor. Then the farmers could plant new crops in the layer of rich, damp soil created. Over the years, layer upon layer of soil has built up in the floodplain, creating one of the most fertile strips of land in the world. Since the completion of the Aswan Dam in 1971, however, this annual flooding has stopped.

Ptolemy made this remarkably accurate map of the course of the River Nile almost 2,000 years ago.

10

The Nile is compared to a lotus plant by many Egyptians – the floodplain as the stem, the delta as the flower and the Faiyoum Oasis as the bud. The Faiyoum area is not a true oasis, because it receives its water supply by canal from the Nile. There are, however, other true oases in the desert, where water can be pumped to the surface and crops can be grown, for example, the Bahariya and Siwa oases. True oases are usually large, heavily populated areas, where intensive farming takes place.

A donkey is used to carry a crop load. Farming methods along the fertile Nile valley have not changed for many centuries.

HOW AN OASIS IS FORMED

An oasis is formed when rain falls on mountains, often many hundreds of miles from the oasis itself. The water then seeps underground along porous rock (rocks that will soak up water) until it passes close enough to the surface for a well to be dug to draw up the water, as in the diagram below.

Rain on mountains

Mountains

Desert

Well to draw up water

Oasis

Impermeable rock (will not allow water through)

Porous rock (allows water through)

Impermeable rock (will not allow water through)

This canal, which comes off the River Nile, feeds precious water to thirsty crops in the region. The Nile is the source of all life in Egypt.

THE KHAMSIN

The Khamsin is a hot, dry wind which blows occasionally from the desert around April, carrying with it red dust and sand. When this wind blows, temperatures can rise by as much as 20 °C in a matter of hours. Paint can be blasted from cars, crops destroyed and roads blocked. The ancient Greek historian Herodotus wrote of an army 50,000 strong, which set out to attack the oasis of Siwa in the Western Desert. The Khamsin blew up and the army was buried under sand and never heard of again.

Sometimes the dust is carried so high that it ends up in countries many thousands of miles from Egypt. The Khamsin can also pick up frogs and fishes and deposit them many miles away.

CLIMATE

Egypt's climate, like its landscape, is typified by extremes, since it lies in one of the hottest and driest regions in the world. The only area with reliable rainfall is a narrow strip, some 80 kilometres wide, on the Mediterranean coast. Even here the annual rainfall is less than 200 millimetres per year, compared to a world average of around 850 millimetres. The hot sun can soon evaporate the little rain that does fall, with daily summer temperatures in Alexandria regularly reaching 30 °C.

Further south, average temperatures increase and average rainfall decreases. In Cairo, the average rainfall is only between 22–24 millimeters each year, while in Aswan, in the far south, the official rainfall is just 1 millimetre per year! Here it is not unusual to have daily temperatures of 42 °C or more. It is estimated that over a quarter of the Nile's water is lost through evaporation as it passes through Egypt.

The people of Egypt

Below (top)
Daily life for
Egyptians over
2,000 years ago.
This is a painting
from an ancient
tomb in Thebes.

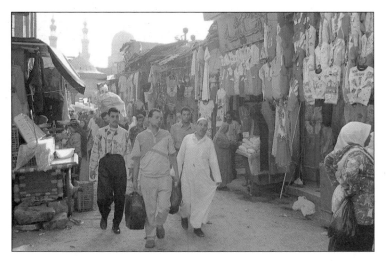

Above (bottom) Modern
daily life in Cairo. Many
Egyptians make their
living in the colourful
markets of the old town.

'Soldiers! Forty centuries are looking down on you!'
– Napoleon Bonaparte, addressing his troops as they stood
below the pyramids, preparing to invade Cairo.

Egyptians have never been far from the frontline of world history, and for many thousands of years they were the most powerful people in the world. To find the first people who populated Egypt, however, we must look further back. Between 10,000 and 20,000 years ago, a change in climate caused the green and fertile plains of North Africa to turn into dust. The peoples of these plains moved to the few remaining rivers, of which the Nile was by far the most important. The peoples began to group together, surviving on hunting, fishing, and gathering nuts and fruit.

Around 7,000 years ago grain and farming skills were brought to the area by peoples from Arabia and Asia. Improved farming methods, combined with the ever-present sun and the life-giving waters of the Nile, allowed great towns and cities to grow and prosper. Soon the ancient Egyptian civilization was as magnificent as any that had come before or was to come after. While Europe was peopled by Stone Age hunters, Egyptians had learned to bake bread, brew beer and glaze pottery. They had also learned to build magnificent pyramids and temples, some of the most stunning architecture the world is ever likely to see.

13

ANCIENT EGYPTIANS AND STAR DEVOTION

It is well known that the sun held a special place in the religon of the ancient Egyptians. What is less well known, but becoming increasingly accepted, is that the Egyptians' religious beliefs were also very much centred on the stars. Detailed star maps were used as guidance for the important points of a person's life, such as birth, coming of age and death.

In fact, it is now believed by many that the Pyramids of Giza and the surrounding area were deliberately positioned so that each pyramid represented a star in the constellation of Orion. The River Nile, which flows next to the pyramids, represented the Milky Way, which follows a similar pattern to the route of the Nile in the night sky next to Orion.

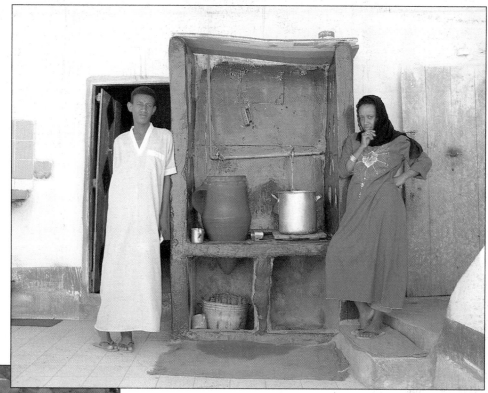

Left The Pyramids of Giza were built in about 2600 BC for the pharaohs Khufu, Khafra and Menkaura. The three smaller pyramids were for their queens.

Right A Nubian couple who live in the south of Egypt.

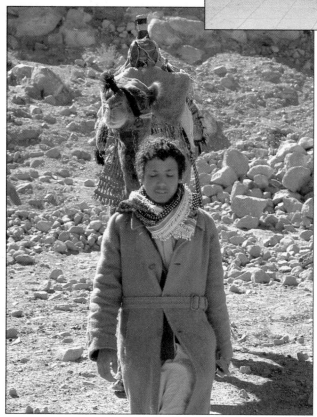

Above A Bedouin man leads his camel.

The ancient Egyptian civilization began to break up about 3,000 years ago, and a succession of other peoples moved in to claim their share of the riches brought by the Nile. In turn, Ethiopia, Persia, Greece, Rome, Arabia, Turkey and Britain took control. Each added their own 'flavour' to the Egyptian culture. The country finally became independent in 1936.

The Egyptians are therefore a very mixed people. The biggest influence is Arabic, and there are close connections with the Middle East. However, there is a definite African feel to the population. Towards the north, people are more European in their outlook, especially in the city of Alexandria, the 'pearl' of the Mediterranean. Towards the south are the dark-skinned Nubians. In the deserts are isolated groups of desert people, the Bedouin. While some still wander the deserts, grazing their goats and selling goods, most have now settled in villages, towns and cities.

RELIGION	
Muslim	89%
Coptic Christian	10%
Others	1%
(including Roman Catholic, Church of England and Hindu)	

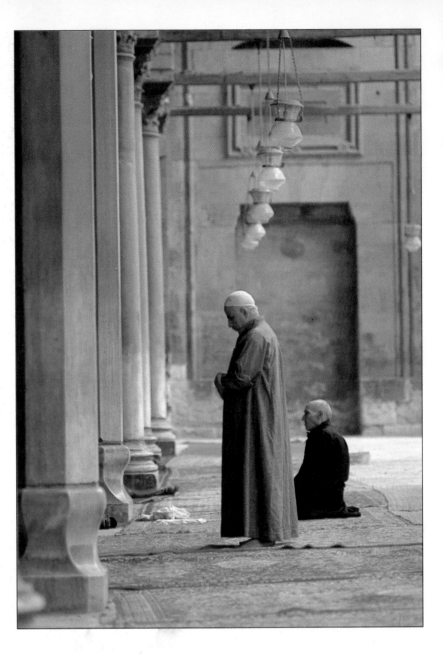

Muslims at prayer in Cairo.

There is also a big difference between Egypt's cities and its villages, where life is slower and more traditional. In many ways, rural life has not changed for thousands of years.

In general, Egyptians are warm, friendly, open and inquisitive. They are also generally religious, and the main religion, Islam, knits the people together. Islam is based on the words of God as written down by the prophet Mohammed, in a book called the Qu'ran (pronounced Ko-raan). Its influence is everywhere. During Ramadan, a holy festival around April each year, nobody eats during daylight hours. When darkness comes, streets are closed to traffic. Candles and lanterns are brought out and people eat, drink (not alcohol, which is forbidden to Muslims), talk and laugh together until the early hours of the morning. This happens every day for a month.

Prayer in Egypt is very important. Here, Muslims bow down and worship towards the holy city of Mecca, in Saudi Arabia.

If you were to walk down any street in Egypt, you would be likely to see women in 'purdah'– wearing headscarves, veils and long gowns to cover their heads, arms and legs. This is how the Qu'ran says they should dress.

Prayer is also very important. At each of the five prayer times every day, you will hear the 'call to prayer'. From the minarets of all the mosques in Egypt will come a wailing chant by the muezzim: 'Allah O Akbar' ('God is Great.'). Then buses, taxis and cars come to a halt. People in shops, offices and building sites will stop their work. They will then lay down a small carpet towards the holy city of Mecca in the east, kneel down and say their prayers to God.

17

The Nubians

Nubians live in the southernmost part of Egypt and the northern half of Sudan. In ancient Egypt, this area was the first Upper Egyptian province, and was called *Ta-Seti,* meaning 'country of the Nubians'. The area has always been rich and fertile, and in ancient times, crocodiles, hippopotami, elephants, lions and panthers would all roam here. The area was also rich in minerals. In fact, the name Nubia, comes from the ancient Egyptian word *'nebu'* or *'nub'*, meaning gold.

Over thousands of years of isolation, the dark-skinned Nubians have developed their own unique culture and language. They are a proud race with high morals, considered by many to be the most gentle and peace-loving of Egyptians. Nubian life is relaxed and carefree. Villages are spotlessly clean, the spacious and airy mudbrick houses always freshly painted. They survive on herding and growing crops using simple methods.

However, their peaceful lives have now been shattered by the building of the Aswan Dam. The 500 kilometre-long Lake Nasser, which was created behind the dam, has engulfed most of the Nubians' land. For most, the old way of life has now gone, as they try to come to terms with the new, soulless concrete settlements built for them by the government.

Above *Village life in Nubian villages is traditional..*

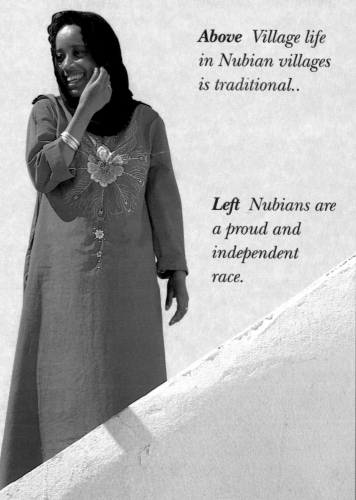

Left *Nubians are a proud and independent race.*

18

In the city

'If I hadn't come here, I couldn't possibly have imagined anything of what it's really like.'
– *American tourist, on seeing Cairo for the first time.*

Cairo by night. This huge, modern city is home to nearly 16 million people.

Egypt is dominated by Cairo, its capital city and centre for trade and government. With a population of 16 million, Cairo contains over a quarter of the population of Egypt. It is also the largest city in Africa.

The first impression of Cairo for many is of sheer amazement. This has been the reaction of tourists visiting Cairo since the city was first established by conquering Arabs in AD 641. Cairo can no longer boast of being the greatest city on earth, but it has managed to keep something of the grandness and elegance for which it was world famous.

Cairo today, however, is a city of confusion. Constant noise, traffic, fumes and concrete, and people of all shapes, sizes, colours and dress, fill every corner of the city streets, day and night. Cairo has the constant air of a city recovering from a major disaster – yet it all works. The city has a feeling of life, exitement and mystery, which is difficult to match anywhere in the world.

THE CAIRO 'QUAKE'

Years of overcrowding and unsafe illegal housing finally caught up with Cairo when, on 12 October 1992, an earthquake shook the city.

Although only medium strength, measuring 5.9 on the Richter Scale, the earthquake caused widespread death and destruction. Many of the older areas of the city were flattened, 600 people were killed, and 10,000 more were injured. The worst damage was in the slum areas, where many buildings collapsed like packs of cards. The biggest to fall was a fourteen-storey block of flats where four storeys had been added illegally by its occupants.

Cairo is growing rapidly, with people flooding into the city in search of a new life at the rate of 5,000 people per week. In 1960, fewer than two out of every five Egyptians lived in cities. Now the figure is four out of every five, and a third of these live in Cairo. The city cannot cope with this population explosion. There are not enough jobs, houses, schools and hospitals for the millions recently arrived from the villages, and not enough money to clear the waste and rubbish they produce. The result is a life of poverty, hunger and filth for many.

Cairo has a fascinating mix of poor and rich, traditional and modern. A vast building plan in the 1960s has created thousands of huge, concrete blocks of flats, which now dominate the city skyline. In among these are the minarets of countless mosques, many over 1,000 years old. Amongst the concrete and mosques there are two lifestyles. One is luxurious and ultra-modern, typified by international hotels where the super-rich show off their wealth. At night the rich return to plush penthouse flats or huge detached houses, where security guards patrol and cooks, maids, servants and gardeners await their next instructions.

Alexandria is Egypt's second-largest city after Cairo. Like Cairo, modern buildings in Alexandria look over the older parts of the city.

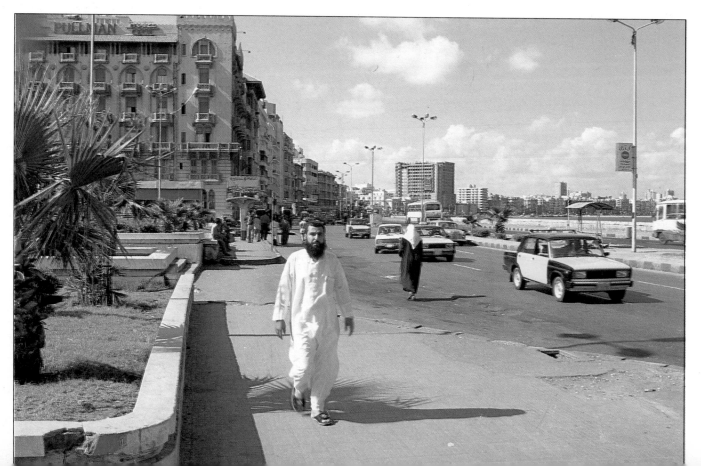

The other side of Cairo is traditional and poor, such as Al-Fustat, or Old Cairo. Here, large families live cramped next to each other in run-down one or two-room flats, often with no toilet or running water. It is common to see parents and their children looking for rotten food on huge piles of rubbish, where hospitals have also dumped their infected waste. Often, village ways are brought into the city, so farming plots, goats and buffaloes fight for space among the tower blocks.

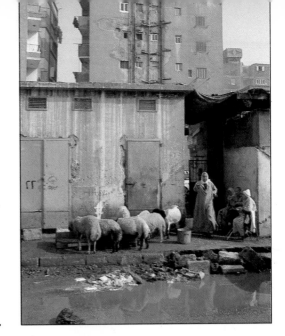

Right *Rural migrants in a poor district of Cairo.*

Living in the City of the Dead

The northern and southern cemeteries of Cairo are together called the 'City of the Dead', because the tombs are not just gravestones, but solid brick buildings with courtyards.

Fatima Rashad el-Bayoumi is one of over half a million people who live here. But this is not a recent thing. As long ago as the fifteenth century, poor Cairenes were living in these luxury homes for the dead.

The Egyptian government has at last accepted the cemeteries as a living area and has supplied them with electricity and water. However, their population is still rising.

A cemetery dweller stands outside his unique home.

'I wish people could make better livings in their villages. There's no more peace and quiet here. Too many people moving in, you see – especially here in the tombs. Families keep inviting more cousins, and everyone just settles in.'
– Fatima Rashad el-Bayoumi, a woman living with her family in the City of the Dead, Cairo.

Source: *National Geographic*, April 1993

'I work for my elder brother making mouse traps. In the morning I go to school with my other brother. In the afternoon we work for five to six hours. The money we make supports our family. I would prefer to concentrate on school and play, but at least I know I will have a job when I grow up.'
– Ahmed, a child worker.

There is a similar division in the workplace. Many poor Cairenes work long hours in tiny workshops, in hot, dirty and cramped conditions. Most of these workers produce tourist goods for sale in the local markets. If they cannot find work here they will do 'odd jobs' such as shoe shining or 'car minding' for poor pay, to avoid the unemployment that can spell disaster and eventual homelessness for them and their families. Many of these workers are children, who have to work in order to help support their families rather than go to school.

Above This boy and his brother can sometimes make 100 mousetraps in one day. They will sell them for the equivalent of 40 pence each.

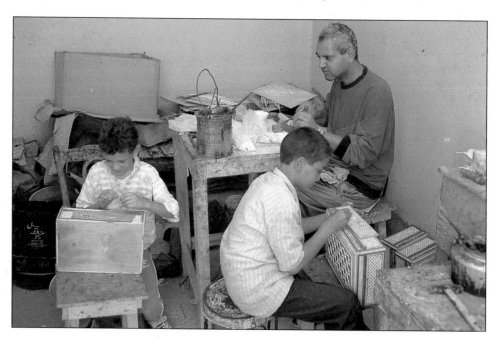

Right Children like these work long hours for low pay in tiny workshops.

Organized Child Beggars

One of the fastest-growing rackets in Cairo is child begging. Children as young as five or six, occasionally with limbs deliberately cut off to increase sympathy, work a 'patch' of the city in groups of five or ten. They are usually ruled over ruthlessly by a teenage boy, himself a former beggar. He will claim a share of the takings in return for keeping the 'patch' clear of other beggars.

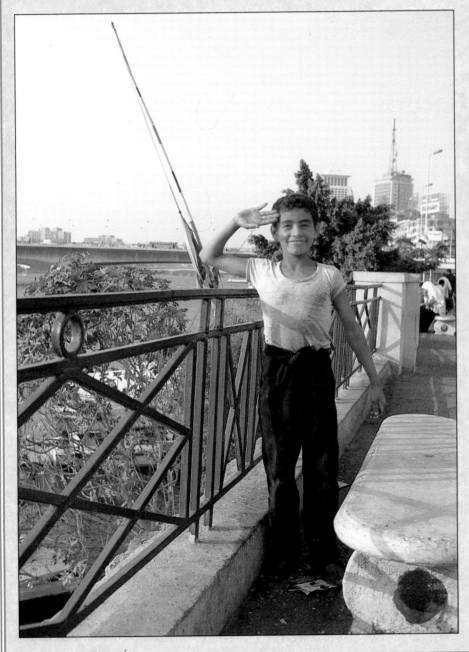

'I am lucky. My brother got a job on a working felucca and now I work for him. Before, I had to sell paper handkerchiefs on the street and ask for money to help my family survive. I would like to go to school, but I have to work to help the family. One day I will be a felucca captain.'
– Mohammed, a former child beggar.

Young children with no money and few prospects, like this young boy, are often pulled into a life of crime.

In contrast are the huge modern factories, such as the steelworks in Helwan, some 50 kilometres from Cairo. Here, and in similar factories, the latest computerized technology is used to sell goods, not only to Egyptians, but to all over the world.

Egypt's second city is Alexandria, a modern industrial city of over 4 million people. Alexandria is also the most popular seaside resort for Egyptians. It is by far the largest city on the Nile Delta and is Egypt's most important port, handling 80 per cent of the country's imports and exports.

'Alexandria is a good city. The air is clean and the sea good. Everybody from Cairo likes to come here. It is not the desert like most of Egypt.'
– Nermeen Hallal, resident of Alexandria.

Cairo Boat People

Ramshackle houseboats along the banks of the Nile provide homes for many of the recently arrived fellahin (farmers) from the villages. They are overshadowed by the towering modern hotels of the tourists, from whom the boat people can earn a basic living. Each boat is 3–6 metres long, and can house families as big as eight or nine, under plastic or canvass covers. Many boat people will spend the day fishing in the polluted waters of the Nile, cooking their catch on open fires on the boat.

Boats like these house some of the families recently arrived from the countryside.

'We travel up the Nile from a village south of Cairo on our boats to fish. We live here on the banks of the river while we are fishing, and bring our families with us. We have a ready market here in Cairo and get a better price for the fish. We also have family back in the country, and go back to help on the land when we are needed.'
– Abdullah Ibrahim, Cairo boat person.

In the countryside

Although only one in five Egyptians now live in the countryside, it is the countryside that provides most of the nation's wealth. However, the vast majority of the rural population contribute little to the national economy. These are the fellahin, farmers struggling to make a living on small plots of land which they mostly own and farm themselves. Their lifestyle has changed little since the times of the pharoahs. A typical fellahin uses simple tools to grow a variety of subsistence crops which they live on, such as maize and vegetables, as well as a cash crop such as sugar, oranges or bananas, which they can sell in the local market. They will have a donkey or buffalo to plough the fields and carry loads, goats for meat and milk, and chickens or pigeons to eat. There is no space to grow fields of grass to graze cattle, so cattle are kept in the village and fed on fodder crops brought in from the fields, such as clover.

FARM ANIMALS OWNED BY EGYPTIANS	
Buffalo	2,500,000
Camels	187,000
Cow	3,389,000
Pigs	94,000
Sheep	4,026,000
Goats	4,137,000
Rabbits	6,409,000
Hens or chickens	76,628,000
Pigeons, ducks, geese or turkeys	24,438,000

'Farming is a good life if you own land. The day is long, using all the hours of sunlight and more, with the whole family involved in various activities. Children herd goats and cattle. Women work with men in the fields. Life is simple with few modern facilities. A wealthy farmer may have a tractor, a pick-up truck, or a water pump for irrigation, but for many, life has not changed since the time of the pharaohs.'
– **Mohammed Shorbagy, villager, El Abaadeia, El Faiyûm Oasis.**

A fellahin proudly stands in front of his crop.

Cattle-driven water pumps like this sakia have been used in Egypt since the times of the pharaohs.

In such a dry land, irrigation of the fields is essential. In fact 99 per cent of farmland has to be irrigated, or the crops would soon wither and die in the hot sun. Water is usually brought up from the Nile using simple pumps, driven by cattle. Nowadays, however, there is an increasing number of farmers using more efficient diesel pumps. Farmers living further from the Nile can use water from a network of canals or wells, built by the government to extend the area of land that can to be farmed.

Until the Aswan Dam was completed in 1970, the fellahin lived in constant fear of flooding, since nearly all of their fields are below the level of the Nile. Now, the highest flood waters can be controlled to allow a steady flow of water into the Nile and its canals, by opening and closing gates in the Aswan Dam and a series of smaller dams down the river. Similarly, the devastating droughts that dried up crops and caused heartbreaking famine are now a thing of the past. Regular watering means that two or more crops can be grown in a year.

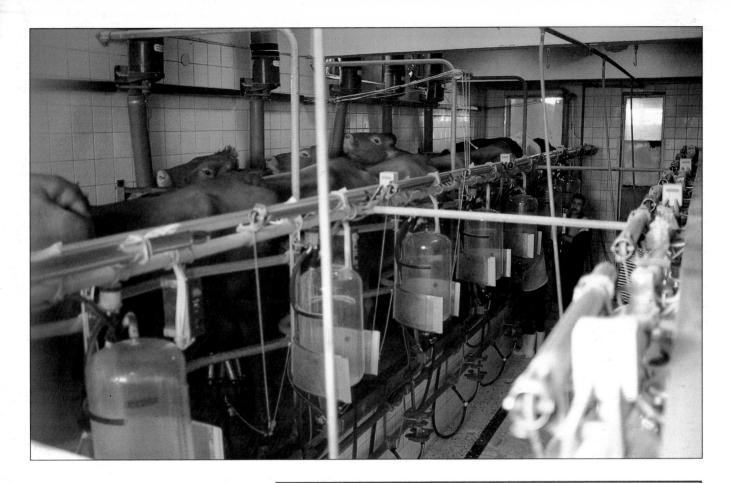

The government-owned farms use the latest technology. Here, a modern milking parlour needs only one worker to operate it.

<table>
<tr><td colspan="3">EGYPT'S AGRICULTURE</td></tr>
</table>

Main goods produced:

Summer	Winter	Summer and winter
Cotton, rice, maize	Wheat, clover, beans	Fruit, potatoes and other vegetables

Farming plots less than 2 hectares:	54%
Farming plots greater than 40 hectares:	6.5%
Percentage of Egypt's food imported:	60%

The simple farming methods used in the fellahin farms contrast with the high technology used in some of the huge farms which thrive in the floodplain. These are usually government-owned, but most of the food they produce does not go to the people. Instead it is sold abroad to help to pay off some of the foreign debt for projects like the Aswan Dam. Oddly enough, the money is also used to buy in food for the people, such as wheat. The government can get more food by selling cash crops such as cotton, and then using the money to buy wheat, than it can using the land to grow wheat in the first place.

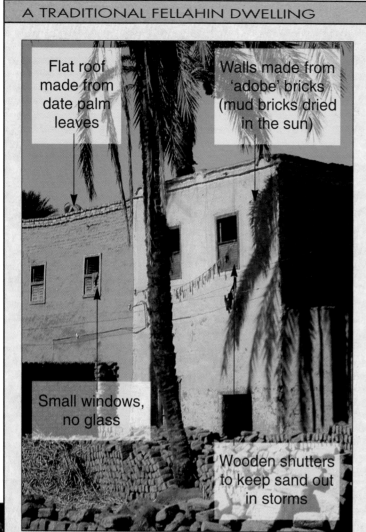

Flat roof made from date palm leaves

Walls made from 'adobe' bricks (mud bricks dried in the sun)

Small windows, no glass

Wooden shutters to keep sand out in storms

Life for most people in the countryside is very traditional. Men work in the fields during the day, usually on their own land, but sometimes on rented land, or as a labourer on one of the huge modern farms. In the evening they sit talking with friends. The women cook, clean and care for the children, but often also help the men in the fields. Old people are cared for within the family, and many generations, including aunts and uncles, can live in the same family home.

Below A farmer and his son return from the market. Extra goods produced on the farms are taken to the local market to be sold as cash crops.

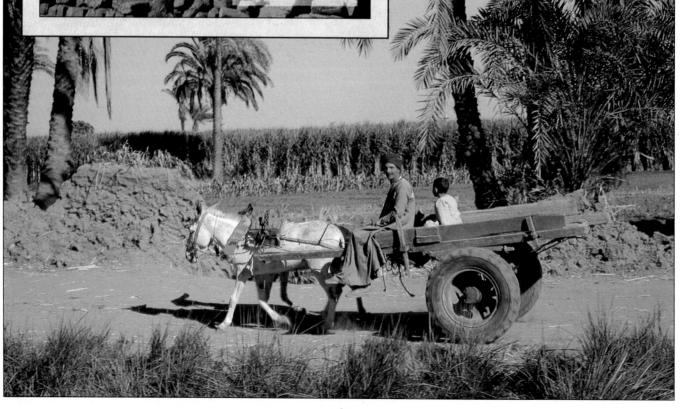

28

The gap between the few rich landowners and the many poor fellahin has been growing steadily larger. Worried by their poverty, the fellahin have been continuing to have large families. Children are often expected to help on their parents' farm, rather than go to school. With no education to better themselves, it has become even more difficult to break out of their poverty. Under Qu'ranic law (the law of Islam), land must be divided amongst the children. With an average family size of five to seven, this means that farm size is getting smaller and smaller. Many young people choose to leave their villages and risk unemployment in the cities, rather than face a life of inevitable struggle and hardship if they stayed in the countryside.

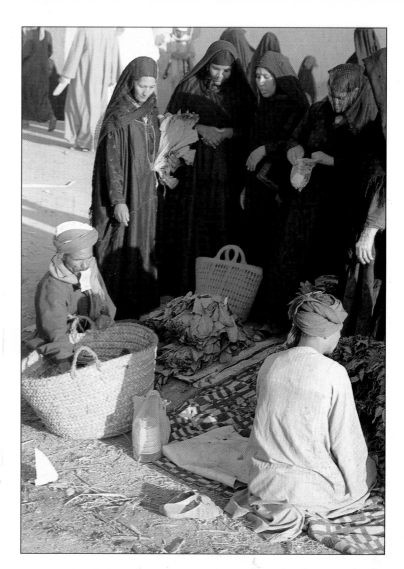

DRESS IN THE RURAL AREAS

Women in the countryside are beginning to return to more traditional types of dress. Full 'purdah', as demanded by the strict Islamic leaders, expects women to cover every inch of their bodies except their eyes when they go out. The difficulties of working in the fields have always meant that women in the past have restricted their purdah to long dresses and colourful headscarves. Now a new trend is developing to wear a huge scarf that covers everything but the face, down to the waist. 'I wear this scarf because it is true Islam', says Fatma, a young village woman. Even more extreme is the 'negab', a tent-like cloak which covers the whole body, but this is even more impractical to work in. As Fatma says, 'you cannot work and wear the negab.'

The souk, *or local market, is not only the place to buy and sell food and other goods. It is also where people come to meet friends and chat.*

Although the desert may look uninhabited, it is actually home to a small number of Bedouin people. These people are generally herders of sheep and goats, travelling from one place to another in search of good pasture.

The ways of the Bedouin have changed much, however. Most now use cars and trucks rather than camels, and though they will travel with their animals at certain times of the year, they often have houses and sometimes businesses in towns and cities.

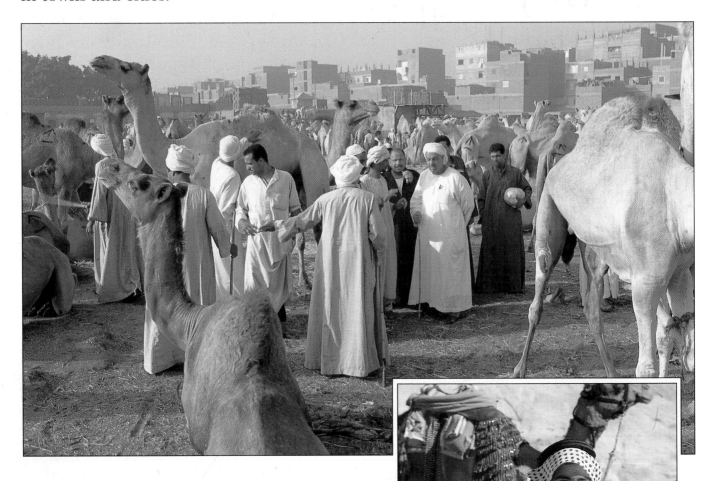

Above *Bedouin at a camel market. Camels are big business in Egypt. A good camel can cost over US$800.*

Right *Life for the Bedouin is rapidly changing. Many are exchanging their wandering lifestyle for a life in the city.*

Why is Egypt poor?

Of all the problems faced by Egyptians, overpopulation caused by rapid population growth is the worst. Overpopulation both causes poverty and is a cause of it. If the government is too poor to give parents help when they need it, for instance when they are old or sick, then they will rely instead on a large family to give them that help. So why is the government so poor?

An Egyptian farmer with his family of six children. The fellahin face a constant struggle to feed themselves and their families.

HISTORICAL REASONS

Since ancient times, Egypt has been colonized, or occupied by many different peoples. Of these, the last were the British.

From 1882–1936, the British were in control of Egypt. During this time there was some increase in wealth, due particularly to an increased production of cotton. However, this wealth was not used to improve the lives of the Egyptian people. Britain saw Egypt as a place to produce cheap, raw materials (such as cotton) for British factories, and as a market where the goods produced in those factories could be sold. The result was that while farming and plantations were encouraged, industry – factories to make goods – was largely forbidden. Egyptians were not allowed to make and sell the

EGYPT COMPARED TO DEVELOPED COUNTRIES 1994			
	EGYPT	BRITAIN	USA
Population (millions)	55	57.7	255.4
Population per km²	58	238	27
Population under 15 years	37.9%	19.7%	21.9%
Averge family size	4.9	2.8	2.6
Life expectancy (years)	61.5	76.5	76
Literacy rate of adults	48.4%	99%	99%
Birth rate (per 1000, per year)	31.3	13.9	15.9
Death rate (per 1000, per year)	9.1	11.5	8.9
Gross Domestic Product (GDP) per head (US$)	630	17,760	23,119

Source: Economist World Statistics, 1995

31

products themselves, only to produce the raw materials. Children were denied higher education so that they would find it difficult to develop industry for themselves. As a result, Egypt has never been able to catch up with the factories of wealthy industrialized countries, even after independence in 1936. When much of the best floodplain land was turned over to growing cotton, many farmers lost their livelihood and became landless labourers, working instead for the British and a few rich Egyptian landowners.

Below (top)
President Nasser is cheered by Egyptians after he managed to win a bloodless victory in the Suez Crisis of 1956.

THE SUEZ CRISIS

The Suez Canal is a vital source of income for Egypt. This is because it is by far the quickest route by sea from Europe to the Middle East or further east. It is a particularly important route for oil tankers, and fees paid by these and other boats provide the Egyptian government with over US$2 billion each year.

This is why the Suez Crisis of June 1956 was such an important event in Egypt's history. Until this time, the canal had been owned by France and Britain. In 1956, President Nasser put the canal under Egyptian control. He wanted the fees from passing boats to pay for the building of the Aswan Dam.

Britain and France were furious, and with Israel they launched an attack on Egypt. The USA and the Soviet Union stepped in to bring peace, and forced the three attackers to withdraw. Nasser had won a famous victory, and his popularity in Egypt and all the Arab world was assured.

Above The Suez Canal, watched over by soldiers in the Crisis of 1956.

NATIONAL DEBT

With such a rapidly growing population, the farms and factories of Egypt have not been able to provide all the goods demanded by its people. So Egypt has had to buy goods from overseas. To do this it must use foreign currency borrowed from Europe and the USA. Egypt also had to borrow money to pay for huge development schemes, such as the Aswan Dam, and for expensive and disastrous wars with Israel in 1967 and 1973. All this borrowing has meant that much of the money Egypt makes from selling goods abroad has to be given straight back to Europe and the USA, just to pay the interest on the national debt. It is estimated that in 1991, Egypt owed nearly US$40 billion.

EGYPT'S TRADE BALANCE

Despite attempts at development, Egypt's trade balance continues to be in the 'red'. What this means is that Egypt is having to buy in more goods from overseas countries (like the USA and Japan) than it is selling back to them. If, for example, Egypt buys US$10 billion worth of goods from abroad, but can only sell goods abroad to the value of $6 billion, its trade balance is in the 'red' – it has a 'trade deficit' of US$4 billion. This is a problem for Egypt as it then does not have enough money to pay off national debts or to buy new goods from overseas, so it has to borrow more. Between 1990–91, nearly half of Egypt's payments overseas were to pay off national debt.

Source: *Barclays Abecor Country Report*

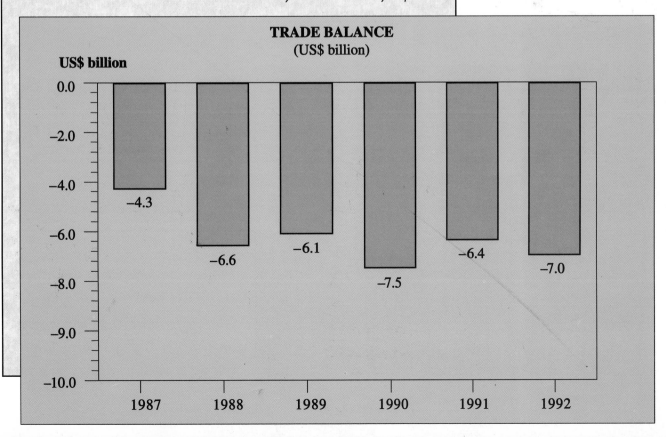

TRADE BALANCE
(US$ billion)

ISLAMIC FUNDAMENTALISM

In recent years, many Egyptian people have wanted to return to strict Islamic laws, such as 'purdah' for all women, banning of all alcohol and gambling, and much stricter punishment for all crimes. These people are called Islamic fundamentalists.

The fundamentalists are growing in number and strength. The government has tried to reduce their power, and the fundamentalists have reacted with violence, carrying out terrorist actions such as bombings and shootings, aimed at factories and tourists. Some foreign tourists, as well as many locals, have been killed as a result of these actions. Pictures of these atrocities have been flashed around the world's television screens and as a result, far fewer tourists and industrialists are willing to come and spend their money in Egypt. High unemployment and billions of dollars in lost revenue have been the result.

THE GOVERNMENT AND THE FUNDAMENTALISTS

Following a period of terrorist action which left some tourists dead and others cancelling their holidays to Egypt, the government decided to crack down on the Islamic fundamentalists, who were demanding stricter religious laws. In March 1993, security agents shot fourteen terrorists dead during eight raids in Cairo, and one on a mosque in Aswan. There were also four members of the security forces killed, as well as three members of the terrorists' families.

Egyptian tourist officials were particularly worried at the possible effect on tourism in Aswan, a quiet town in the south of the country, as yet unaffected by the violence.

Following these events, seven terrorists were executed in Cairo Prison on 8 July 1993.

Political extremism is not a new thing in Egypt. In 1983, these Islamic fundamentalists were put on trial for trying to overthrow the government.

34

The 'Forgotten' Bedouin Peoples of the Sinai

In the Sinai Desert, not far from the Rafah border post with Israel, there is a large camp. It is a basic set of shelters made from cardboard, branches and plastic, giving little protection from the cold night winds and rain of the North Sinai Coast.

These shacks house what remains of the Bedouin Mahalha people, forced to leave their traditional grazing land in Gaza, south Israel after the Israelis withdrew from the Sinai in 1982. Now they are left with no land to call their own. Since Israel has refused to allow them in, and Egypt has claimed to be unaware of their existence, it seems that the people's chances of seeing their families again are slim.

We are Palestinians, I was born near Beersheba [now in Israel]. I fled to Gaza during the first [1948] war. Now we wait here to rejoin our families in the Gaza.'
— Tenkiya Saleem, one of the oldest members of the Mahalha people.

EGYPT AND THE GULF WAR

Egypt was one of the few countries to actually make a profit out of the Gulf War in 1990. Egypt sent an armed force to help countries such as the USA and Britain free Kuwait from the Iraqis, who had invaded their country. In return for this, US$7 billion was wiped off the massive national debt owed to the USA by Egypt.

Palestinian refugees like these wait patiently to be allowed to return to their homes in the Gaza Strip, now part of Israel.

Development in Egypt

The Egyptian government knows its people face many problems, but it is difficult to find how to solve them. The government cannot afford to solve all Egypt's problems, so where should it spend the little money that is available? There has been much development in Egypt, and much of it has been right at the forefront of modern technology.

ENERGY

Egypt uses many different types of energy to power its homes, offices, shops and factories. These energy sources can also provide much-needed funds.

Oil, first discovered under the sea-bed in the Gulf of Suez in 1896, has become a vital energy source for the Egyptian government. In 1993, 46 billion tonnes of oil was produced (nearly 1 million barrels per day). As well as providing power for its people, the money from oil sales has helped to pay off some of Egypt's huge debts. There are two problems with this, however. The oil will run out in eighteen years if Egypt continues to use it at the present rate. Also, since oil prices dropped in the 1980s, other countries have been paying far less for Egyptian oil. Therefore the government has been making a smaller profit.

DEVELOPMENT OF AQUA PARK

One of the biggest growth industries in Egypt is the tourist industry. 'Aqua Park' is a swimming-pool complex which has been built recently in the desert a few kilometres outside Cairo. Here rich Egyptians and tourists lounge in coffee bars, sun patios, or next to the pool, plummet down breathtaking water-slides 150 feet high, or enjoy the modern pools and wave machine. Unlike many similar developments in richer countries of the world, Aqua Park can claim to have one major advantage – almost unlimited sunshine!

Aqua Park, one of the many tourist developments built to satisfy the demands of rich Egyptians.

Right The Aswan Dam is over 3.5 kilometres wide. At its base, the wall is nearly 1 kilometre thick.

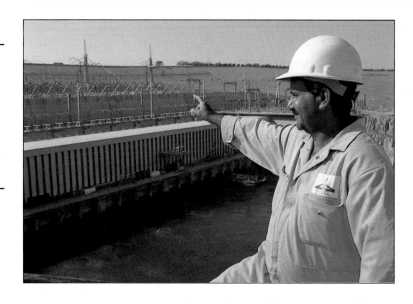

An important alternative to oil is natural gas, which has been found in vast quantities in the Nile delta and the Western Desert. Gas may earn Egypt money in the future.

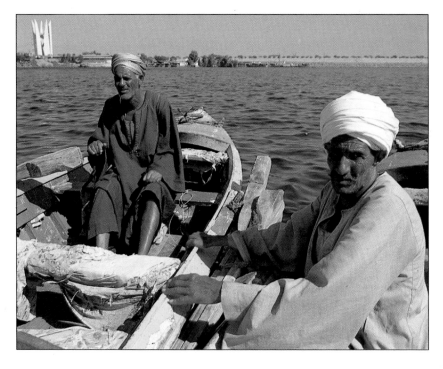

Surprisingly, for a country which has so little rainfall, water has become an important source of energy. The source of this water is the Aswan Dam, completed in 1971. This immense structure took ten years to build. Behind it was formed the largest artificial lake in the world, named Lake Nasser after the then-president of Egypt. The hydroelectric power generated from the dam now makes up 25 per cent of the electricity used in Egypt.

With the building of the Aswan Dam, fishing on the 50 kilometre-long Lake Nasser has become an important industry.

The building of the dam has also brought problems, however. Thousands of Nubians were forced to move from their traditional lands in the fertile area that Lake Nasser now occupies. The silt that used to be spread across the Nile Valley floor during the annual floods now piles up on the floor of Lake Nasser. If no action is taken, in time, this mud will make Lake Nasser unuseable.

NEW CITIES

Overpopulation has caused many problems in established cities, such as Cairo and Alexandria. The government decided that people needed to be attracted away from these centres of growth, so since 1979, new 'desert cities'

have been built. One example is the 10th Ramadan City, where new houses, cleaner air and modern factories have attracted 100,000 people. Over 500 new industries have been drawn by the promise of cheap land, cheap rents and money grants provided by the government. Life is not always easy, however. Workers have to leave their families if they want to work in the new city , and many would prefer to travel two or three hours to work, and remain in the larger cities, rather than move. Many complain that the new city is soulless and isolated, and there are many cases of depression and suicide.

Above Clean air and new houses in a suburb of one of Egypt's new cities.

NEW COMMUNITIES, 22 APRIL 1994

This map shows Egypt's ambitious plan to build new cities. It is hoped that this will ease the growing pressure on existing cities such as Cairo and Alexandria.

MEDITERRANEAN SEA

New Sadat City
10th Ramadan
El Salhia
New Borg el Arab
6th October
15th May

River Nile

RED SEA

KEY
■ New cities already built
□ New cities planned

Cairo has recently spent much money on improving its road system, with new flyovers in the city centre.

DEVELOPING THE CITIES

There have been many attempts over the years to solve the problem of poor living conditions in established cities such as Cairo. Vast tower blocks have been built to house the poor and homeless, and to reduce overcrowding. The building of the Cairo underground, including a 60-kilometre line to the city of Helwan, has shortened traffic queues and reduced pollution in the streets above. New, wider roads and bridges have been built. One-way systems have been developed. Many parts of central Cairo are now connected by flyovers. Billions of dollars have been spent on a new sewage system to improve hygiene, with main sewage pipes that are bigger than a double-decker bus! Drinking water is now cleaner, and disease has been reduced. However, there are still over half a million people living in poverty as squatters in Cairo's City of the Dead, and the city has among the worst traffic accident records in the world, with over 1,000 people killed in some years.

39

Development in Imbaba

Imbaba is one of the poorest areas of Cairo. Here, changes are now taking place which its residents could only have dreamt of five years ago. For some thirty years, the Cairo authorities overlooked this slum area to the northwest of the city. Living conditions had dropped to dangerous levels as a result. With little piped water or drains, death rates from diseases such as diarrhoea were some of the highest in Cairo, especially among the very young. Few medical centres had been built, and even fewer doctors were prepared to work in the district. Overcrowding had reached crisis proportions. Over 600,000 people were crushed into 2 square kilometres of narrow alleys and half-built tower blocks – about one person every 3 square metres.

More were coming from the countryside every week, adding further floors to already crumbling buildings.

At last, perhaps worried that the anger of residents might lead to terrorist activity, the authorities in Cairo finally decided to do something. In the last few years, the main roads have been paved, piped water and sewers supplied to every block, and regular rubbish collection started. A water-purification plant has been set up and a brand-new youth club built. In total US$15 million has been spent to improve the area, and more is planned.

It has been an agonizing wait for the long-suffering residents of Imbaba, but at last conditions are beginning to improve.

'People are willing to wait, if they feel the authorities are listening.'
– **Dr Shahateh, Governor of Imbaba.**

Much of Imbaba is a building site, as Cairo attempts to tackle some of its worst housing problems.

AGRICULTURE

With such a large population and so little fertile land, the production of food has always been one of the priorities of the Egyptian government. That is why so much money has been spent on reclaiming land from the desert, using a complicated system of canals from the Nile. Here, crops such as cotton, potatoes, tobacco and oranges are grown. In these vast fields immense machinery, such as a moving sprinkler on wheels nearly 0.5 kilometres long, operate with hardly any people – an odd situation in a country where so many millions are unemployed. Production has become very efficient: for example, Egypt sells one-third of the total cotton sold in the world today. However, most of the food produced is not available to the hungry people of Egypt. Instead it is sold abroad to help pay off Egypt's national debt.

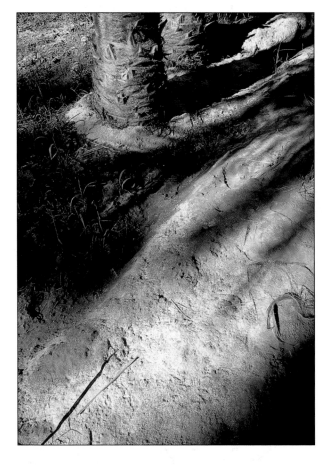

'Whoever ... [cannot] ... feed himself can enjoy neither freedom nor dignity.'
– **President Mubarek, December 1982.**

Above *Land reclaimed from the desert suffers from salinization of the soil, where the soil is so dry from water evaporation that salt rises to the surface.*

Left *Crops like these dates can be grown on land reclaimed from the desert.*

41

The future of Egypt

Egypt's development so far has improved the quality of life of many of its people. Nevertheless, countless problems still exist. As at so many times in its past, Egypt stands at a crossroads. The decisions that the government takes now will dictate whether the improvements are just temporary, or if they can be maintained and Egypt's people can look to the twenty-first century with optimism. But which path should the country take?

Government health clinics advise people to limit the size of their families to help the population problem in Egypt.

'I work in a government clinic, and our role is both to educate people in the need for population control, and in the various methods of achieving it. When we started, we went out into the villages to encourage people to take part. But now they know about us and come directly to the clinic. Slowly we are winning the battle.'
—Sharira El Zayd Ahmet, health clinic worker, Luxor.

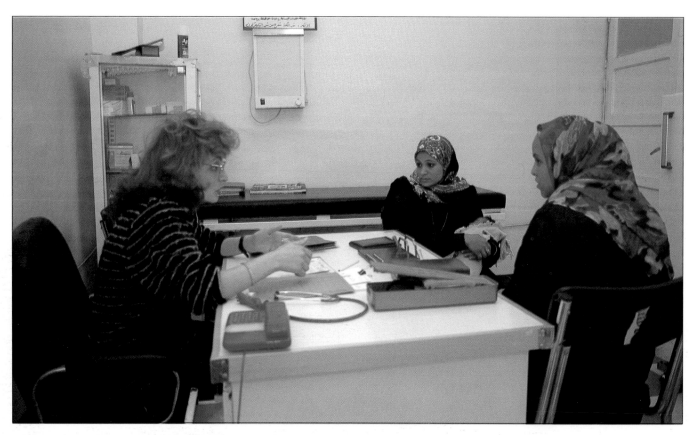

Most people believe that future development depends on a successful population-control programme. The government has been very active in promoting family planning since 1985, when the National Population Council was set up. There has been a big effort to allow women access to birth control facilities, especially in the rural area where the average family has around five children. There has been a media campaign on television, radio and newspapers, encouraging parents to have no more than two children, and warning of the difficulties of having more.

To some extent these efforts have been successful. In 1981, only 25 per cent of women used family planning; by 1991 this figure had nearly doubled. There has been a dramatic reduction in the growth rate of the population from 3 per cent a year in 1985 to 2.2 per cent a year in 1993. However, there are still big problems with reducing population growth in rural areas. Doctors do not like working in the isolated, traditional villages of the countryside, and many of the women in these areas do not find it easy to adopt new customs quickly.

Above *Diagrams on government posters like this one are always made especially clear, since most women in the countryside cannot read.*

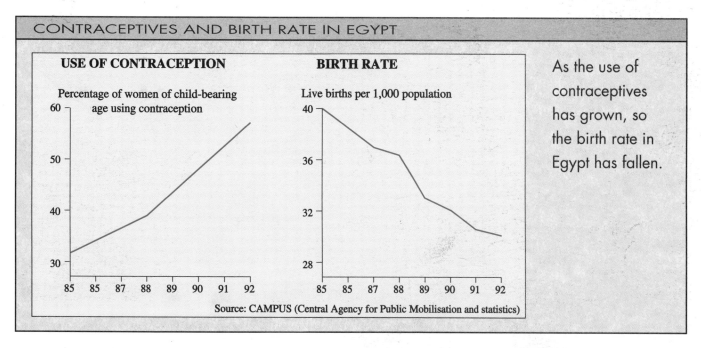

CONTRACEPTIVES AND BIRTH RATE IN EGYPT

USE OF CONTRACEPTION

Percentage of women of child-bearing age using contraception

BIRTH RATE

Live births per 1,000 population

As the use of contraceptives has grown, so the birth rate in Egypt has fallen.

Source: CAMPUS (Central Agency for Public Mobilisation and statistics)

Above Much money has been spent on introducing high technology to Egypt's industry. Egyptian goods are now sold all over the world.

Further development of the desert areas is another option. There is a huge scheme to carry water 150 kilometres from the Nile, to irrigate 250,000 hectares of the land on either side of the Suez Canal. This scheme, and all the other irrigation projects, will depend on the continued supply of water from the River Nile. At the moment, Egypt uses as much Nile water as it is allowed under an agreement with Sudan to the south. Many projects could not go ahead because there is simply not enough water to spare.

Another possible way forward is to use the estimated 25–30 per cent of the country's labour force who currently work in the 'black economy'. This represents the many people who work in small businesses illegally, untaxed and unregistered by the government. Some say that these people should be allowed to work legally. Given loans, grants and other benefits by the government, many of their businesses could become highly profitable.

'Until now, the whole system has been geared to ignoring these small enterprises and pretending they don't exist.'
–Heba Handoussa, Egyptian economics expert.

Right Egypt has caught on to the idea of 'business parks', specially designed industrial estates with factories fully equipped with the latest technology.

High technology has recently become a popular development path. If Egypt can produce high quality electronic goods, it will have an advantage over other producers of hi-tech goods. Its people will work for a fraction of the wages of those in the developed world. With this in mind, the Pyramids Technology Valley (PTV) has been built near Cairo, while two science parks have opened up in the 6th October City.

The majority of Egyptians face all these development paths with a weary fatalism as a result of many years of hardship. The most commonly used word in Egypt is *'inshallah'*, meaning 'if God wills it'. The Egyptian people are eager for change and improvement in the quality of their lives and are prepared to work for it. But if it does not happen, then life must go on!

The future of these children depends on how successfully Egypt continues to develop.

45

Glossary

Barren Unable to grow anything.

Cash Crops Crops grown to sell for money.

Delta A flat, fan-shaped area of land where a river splits into many channels as it empties into the sea.

Energy Sources Sources of power to run machinery in factories, homes and offices.

Exports Goods produced by a country that are sold abroad.

Family Planning Methods used to control the number of children in a family.

Flood Plain The area on either side of a river where the river regularly floods and deposits silt.

Flyovers Roads raised on concrete pillars above the ground.

Fodder Crops Crops grown as food for cattle.

Foreign Debt The amount of money that a country owes to other countries (usually measured in $US).

Gross Domestic Product (GDP) The total amount of money produced by a country's businesses. GDP per head is the Gross Domestic Product divided by the number of people in the country, or the average wealth per person in a country.

Hydroelectric power Electricity made from the power of moving water.

Imports Goods that have to be brought into a country from abroad.

Irrigation The artificial watering of the land, with channels, sprinklers or pipes.

Islam The religion of Muslims, followers of the teachings of the prophet Mohammed.

Literacy rate The proportion of the population who can read or write.

Media Campaign A story of particular point of view reported for an extended length of time by a country's newspapers, radio and television.

National Debt The same as foreign debt.

Oases Fertile places in the desert.

Plantation A large area of land used for growing one or a few crops, usually in order to sell for money.

Purdah Strict dress code for women demanded by many Islamic leaders, where the head, legs and arms have to be covered by long flowing robes.

Reservoir A human-made lake in which water is stored.

Revenue Income received from any source.

Silt Very fine particles of mud and rock carried by a river.

Subsistence Crops Crops grown by farmers to feed their families rather than to sell in local markets.

Further information

ACTIONAID, Hamlyn House, Archway, London N19 5PG, provides information on Egypt and other developing countries.

Egyptian Tourist Office, 168 Piccadilly, London W1V, will provide general information on Egypt.

State of the World's Children is an annual report with information on developing countries, available from UNICEF, 55 Lincoln Inn Fields, London WC2A 3NB.

Locality Studies: Cairo – Four children and their city, a video and resource pack which introduces Cairo through the eyes of four children.

Oxfam, 274 Banbury Road, Oxford OX2 7DZ, will provide information on small-scale development projects in Egypt.

The Development Education Association, 3rd Floor, Cowper Street, London EC2A 4AP can provide information on teaching packs.

The Overseas Development Administration produce a newsletter and general information on development in the developing world.

Books to read

Animal Homes: Deserts by Robert Burton (Belitha Press,1991)
BBC Factfinders: Egypt by Steve and Patricia Harrison (BBC, 1990)
Egypt by Ian Morrison (Heinemann, 1990)
Life in the Deserts by Lucy Baker (Franklin Watts, 1990)
The Nile by Julia Waterlow (Wayland, 1992)

For more advanced readers:

Khul Khaal – Five Egyptian Women tell their Stories by Nayra Atiya (American University in Cairo Press, 1991)

Films

The following films are all documentaries for schools:

Landmarks: Egypt (BBC)
Places and People: Cairo – A growing city (BBC)
Places and People: Cairo – Problems of Growth (BBC)

Index

Numbers in **bold** refer to illustrations.

ancient Egyptians 13, **13**, 14, **14**, 15
animals 21, 25, 30, **30**
architecture 13
Aswan Dam 10, 18, 26, 27, 32, 33, 37, **37**

birth control 42, 43, **43**
birth rate 6, 43
black economy 44
Britain 15, 31, 32, 35

children 22, **22**, 23, **23, 45**
cities 5, 19-24, 38, 39
  Alexandria 12, 24, 38
  Cairo 9, 12, 19-21, 23, 24, 38, 39, 45
  Helwan **5**, 39
  development in 39, **39, 40, 40**
  new cities 38, 45
City of the Dead 21, **21,** 39
climate 8, 12, 13, 26
clothes
  negab 29
  purdah 17, 29, 34
colonization 31
crops 25, 26, 27
  cash 25, 27
  cotton 27, 31, 41
  subsistence 25, 26

deserts 5, 7-12, 30
  Sahara 7
  Sinai 8, 35
  Western 8, 37
drinking water 39, 40

earthquake 19
education 29, 31
energy 36-7
  hydroelectricity 37
  gas 37
  oil 36, 37
  water
Europe 13, 32, 33

factories 24, 31, 33
families 21, 24, 28, 31, **31,** 43
farming 5, 10, 11, 21, 25-9, 31, 33, 41, **41**
  methods 13, 25-7
fellahin (small farmers) 24, 25-9, **25, 28**
felucca 9, **9**
festivals
  Ramadan 16
flag 4
France 32

government 27, 31, 32, 34, 36, 38, 41, 42, 44
Greece 15
Gulf War 35

independence 4, 31
irrigation 26, **26,** 44
Islamic fundamentalism 34, **34**
Israel 8, 32, 33, 35

Japan 33

Khamsin wind 12
Kuwait 35

lakes
  Nasser 9, 18, 37, **37**
  Tana 10
  Victoria 10
landowners 25, 29, 31
landscape 5, 8
law
  Islamic 34
  Qu'ranic 29

Mediterranean Sea 7, 9, 12
minarets 17, 20
mosques 17, 20, 34
Mount Gebel Katherina 5, **7,** 8

national debt 27, 33, 35, 36, 41

Oases 11
  Bahariya 11
  Faiyoum 11
  Siwa 11

pollution
peoples
  Arab 13, 15, 19
  Bedouin 15, **15,** 30, **30,** 35, **35**
  Cairene 21, 22
  Cairo boat people 24, **24**
  Nubian 15, 18, 37
population control 6, 20, 31, 42, 43, **43**
port 24
poverty 5, 6, 20, 21, 22, 29, 31, 33
Pyramids Technology Valley (PTV) 45, **45**
Pyramids of Giza 13, 14, **14**

Qattâra Depression 8, 9

Red Sea 7
religion 14, 16-17, **16, 17**
River Nile 4, 5, 8, 9, 10, 11, 12, **12,** 13, 14, 24, 26
  Delta 9, 24, 37
  sources of 10, **10**
  Valley 8, 37
Rome 15

science parks 45, **45**
steelworks 24
Sudan 9, 18, 44
Suez canal 32, 44
  crisis 32, **32**

technology 24, 25, 26, **26,** 27, **27,** 36, 45
terrorism 34, 40
tourism 19, 22, 24, 34, **36**
trade 33
Turkey 15

USA 32, 33, 35